CW00661405

THE MAMMOTH BOOK OF
SKULLS

EDITED BY ILYA

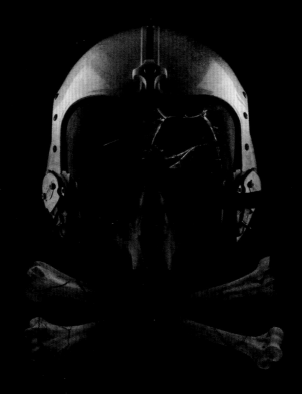

ROBINSON

RUNNING PRESS
PHILADELPHIA · LONDON

ROBINSON

First published in Great Britain in 2014 by Robinson

A CIP catalogue record for this book
is available from the British Library.

UK ISBN: 978-1-47211-150-0 (paperback)
UK ISBN: 978-1-47211-532-4 (ebook)

Designed and typeset in The Sans & The Serif
by Andrew Barron @ thextension
Printed and bound in China by C & C Offset

Robinson
is an imprint of
Constable & Robinson Ltd
100 Victoria Embankment
London EC4Y 0DY

An Hachette UK Company
www.hachette.co.uk

www.constablerobinson.com

First published in the United States in 2014
by Running Press Book Publishers,
A Member of the Perseus Books Group

Books published by Running Press are available at special
discounts for bulk purchases in the United States by corporations,
institutions, and other organizations. For more information, please
contact the Special Markets Department at the Perseus Books
Group, 2300 Chestnut Street, Suite 200, Philadelphia, PA 19103,
or call (800) 810-4145, ext. 5000, or e-mail
special.markets@perseusbooks.com.

US ISBN: 978-0-7624-5463-1
US Library of Congress Control Number: 2014935175

9 8 7 6 5 4 3 2 1
Digit on the right indicates the number of this printing

Running Press Book Publishers
2300 Chestnut Street
Philadelphia, PA 19103-4371

Visit us on the web!
www.runningpress.com

Image on page one: *Mnemic* by Don Clark
www.invisiblecreature.com

CONTENTS

INTRODUCTION

Look around you. Skulls are everywhere. Skull T-shirts, skull clutch bags, skull sweets and toys, skulls in art, skull socks for heck's sake! In seemingly every High Street in every land, everywhere you look – there's a skull, front and centre, teeth bared and insolently grinning.

Why skulls? What is it that has made skull iconography so cool, such a must have? Maybe it's because skulls are like opinions – or else that certain other body part favoured by the proverb – everybody's got one.

Perhaps it is the universality of death, the only certain thing in this life being that it must one day end ...

Skull images have become so ubiquitous that in many instances we are becoming all but oblivious to their ultimate meaning – that most final of all messages. How else, in a recent news clipping, could a respectable young mother be photographed attending the memorial for Lee Rigby, a Guardsman killed in a terrorist attack (The London *Evening Standard*, Thursday 28 May,

Skulls are so in, they're out. "Oh look, it's another skull. Yawn." Last year's thing. Haven't you heard? (What's the new thing? "Hoot! It's owls." Or whatever.)

2013, p7), with her pram – her pram – adorned in wide-mouthed screaming skulls?

Let's talk of graves, of worms, and epitaphs; make dust our paper and with rainy eyes write sorrow on the bosom of the earth
Shakespeare, *Richard II, Act 3, Sc 2*

It is ironic, but it is true – rather than morbid fascination, for many, skulls act as a reminder of life. They are more often a celebration or expression of joy than they are of sadness or sorrow.

"Some people see these [skulls] as signs of death, or the death of a childhood icon, and I don't see them that way at all. For me, they're specimens of life. Looking at bones talks about what happened in life. It's not death and gore. It's the evidence left behind."

– Stephanie Metz interviewed in *Content* Magazine, Issue 5.2, Summer 2013. Original article by Gillian Claus

"I was told by a police officer that people on the street have nothing better to look forward to than death. I decided if that was the case, then maybe death had better step in himself. I've sort of become a parody of death, because rather than taking life, I'm giving it."
Thanatos, Real Life Superhero, whose costume is skillfully skullish

The street festival known as The Day of the Dead (*Día de Los Muertos*), originating in Mexico, has over the course of the last century or so caught on worldwide, in one form or another. That is a very literal response to death, meeting it head on: paying tribute to lost loved ones, welcoming them back to hearth and the family bosom, yet also big-hearted enough not to exclude the

Above
Yale's Skull & Bones society

cadaverous remains of complete strangers who might wander in. Everybody is as busy and populous in death as they ever were in life, and all skeletons are invited to the feast.

Reflect also on Halloween, and how much that has turned into an international holiday, a huge excuse to party and Trick or Treat. Just like superheroic Thanatos, everybody's dressed up as a spook or skeleton. And these days, walking down any street, that same special effect seems to be happening everywhere all year round.

Fashion victims everywhere: every T-shirt in town with a skull emblazoned on it … why, almost enough to fill a picture book compendium!

And you know what? I myself might have been there at Ground Zero, on The Day Skull Tees Took Over. Except that it was night, and we were in a club: London's NAG NAG NAG, the trendiest nightclub in the whole wide world at that very instant, probably. This was, I don't know, somewhere around the winter of 2004 … my memory is hazy, but we had more important things on our minds, like thumping nu electro beats, glitter and vodka mixers. In walks Fil OK, NAG DJ and one-half of the club's house-band Atomizer, wearing a Jolly Roger skull and crossbones tee bought that day from a gift shop attached to the galleon *Golden Hinde II*, a heritage tourist attraction. Nice and simple, white on black iconic design: as worn by pirates. The next week there were six of them – including mine. In the weeks after that, they started to proliferate – if that's not too ironic a term – across the country, and, before long, all around the world. By the following summer every sort of variant was being explored, a global fashion phenomenon that has only grown in height and breadth ever since, from Alexander McQueen, Prada and Ralph Lauren back down to WalMart/George at ASDA and TKMaxx.

So, skulls are everywhere. Zombies now, too.

Could they simply be fulfilling a widespread cultural death wish? (It's called Eschatology). Truly these are the Final Days, the End Times ... or is that nothing more than Baby Boomers' fantasy? Every generation thinks, in its self-obsessed navel-gazing hubris, that it will be the last. The present era's defining demographic are hitting their 60s, and feeling it – and there's more of them around than anyone else!

Or ... who cares. Maybe skulls are huge for no other reason than that they look just so damn HOT! Revel in it ...

ILYA ILLKILLYA, *Dead Ed*

Right
Ya Boo Sucks, Death – photo by Andy Bleck

ART SKULLS

Spanish Surrealist Salvador Dali, the celebrated photographer Irving Penn, Flemish painter Frans Hals, Vincent van Gogh ... so many famous names in the big-A world of Fine Art have, down the centuries, played with and explored the resonance of skull imagery. In the following section we play with and explore alongside a wealth of international talent – tableaux, collage and installation artists and innovators, leaders in their field – names one and all to watch for, now and in the future: some of whom might themselves continue to be talked about in centuries to come.

Top
Ballerina in a Death's Head (1939), Salvador Dali (1904–1989), Oil on canvas, 24.5 x 19.5 cm. Collection Merz/Kunstmuseum Liechtenstein, Vaduz © VG Bild-Kunst, Bonn 2012

Right
The Final Project Jo Spence (1934–1992), Diagnosed with leukemia, her response to the illness was to make more art. "*Up until her* final moments Spence was still probing at the potential of photography to articulate the 'unrepresentable'.'" George Vasey. © Jo Spence Estate, Richard Saltoun Gallery

Opposite, clockwise from top left
Young Man holding a Skull (Vanitas), 1626–28 Franz Hals (1580–1666). National Gallery, London

Kop van een skelet met brandende sigaret, Skull of a Skeleton with Burning cigarette (undated, c.1886) Vincent van Gogh (1853–1890). Van Gogh Museum, Amsterdam

Selbstporträt mit fiedelndem Tod, Self Portrait with Death playing fiddle Arnold Boecklin (1827–1901). Nationalgalerie, Berlin

Ospedale, New York, 1980 Irving Penn (1917–2009) © Condé Nast

TAB. IX

MEXICAN DREAM CATCHER

ISABELLE DALLE

Formerly an art director for *Marie-Claire*, now a freelance artist, Isabelle Dalle lives and works in Paris. Influenced by nature and the human sciences, she uses her imagination to transform the traditional art of medical journals and botanical prints into "digital anatomical portraits".

An ongoing series since 2011, ANATOMY is planned for an eventual total of 78 boards, or "planches", which she then plans to print and reproduce as a tarot-like card game. She tells us, "The hardest thing when you're freelance is the uneven cash flow. Trust in what you do and let your feelings speak. Images are direct, and say more than words."

www.isabelledalle.com
www.isabelledallestore.com

ISABELLE DALLE

Top left
Planche IX.
Série ANATOMY – 2011

Opposite
Planche XVIII.
Série ANATOMY – 2013

Following spread, left
Planche XII.
Série ANATOMY – 2011

Following spread, right
Planche V (noir).
Série ANATOMY – 2011

BIRTH OF THE DEATH

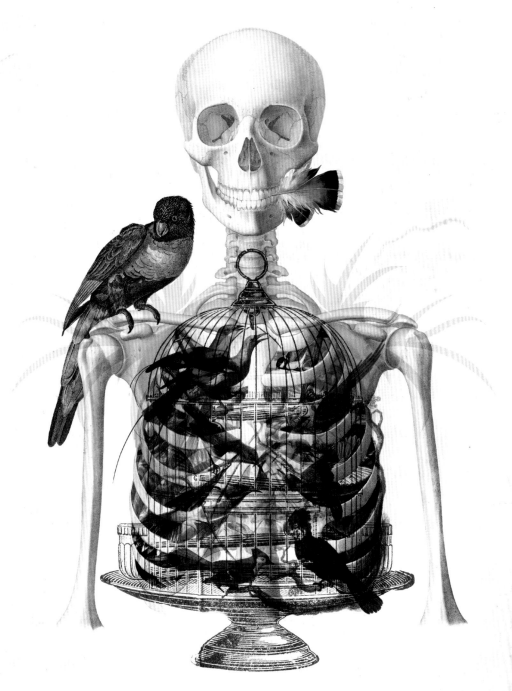

"Happy Bird Day!"

TAB. XII

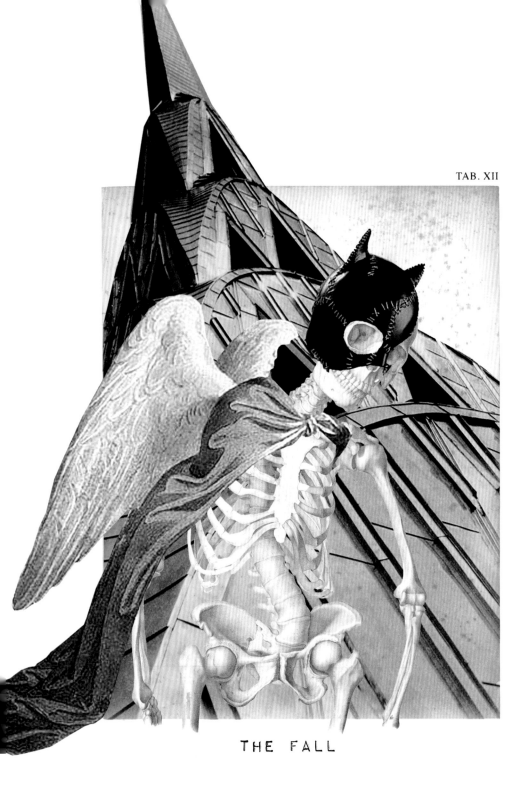

THE FALL

TAB. V

WE BETTER FLY !

JEPH GURECKA

Jeph lives and works out of Brooklyn, New York. He has shown internationally in group and solo exhibitions. Often taking the form and title of Memento Mori (Latin: "Remember that you will die."), Jeph's works, both large and small scale, explicitly reflect the impermanence of the mortal world, absurdity in the moment, the superstitions and desires of society.

Bread, salt and water are the essentials of life, often lending them social, religious, and economic significance – an idea Gurecka explores by using these fundamental resources as media for his sculpture.

Top left
Eating My Demons series
(Bread, salt, water),2002
Archival Pigment Print,
edition of 7
An anatomically correct cast
bread skull was photographed
in the style of Irving Penn's
famous photograph – *Bread,
Salt and Water*. The mould was
made from a real skull.

Opposite
Memento Mori, 2005
Bread, archival resin.
approx. 15 x 10 in.
1,000 anatomically correct
cast human skulls in various
types of bread, archival resin.
Collection of Futura Gallery
and Castle Trebesice, Prague
Czech Republic

The production process – making and baking

Bread, salt and water – sustenance itself: Gurecka experiments
with their physical properties as much as he employs them for
symbolic metaphor. "As material, bread has an amazing organic
process that I attempt to shape, but that ultimately shapes itself.
The level of humidity, ingredients, care and concentration given,
determines how the material will respond. In many ways, it is like
a chemistry experiment."

BETO JANZ

Currently working as an Art Director in his native Brazil, graphic designer and artist Roberto R. Janz (Beto Janz) is a confirmed skull lover. Skateboards, Heavy Metal and his self-confessed Rock'n'Roll lifestyle all contribute to an aesthetic mosh-pit of art and ideas. From underground to corporate, his career forms a nexus point where more than one universe connects. He treats his artwork as integral to his personality – and vice versa – as all good artists should. He always makes his personal mark.

Based in Curitiba, Brazil, he's currently looking for opportunities to work abroad.

www.betojanz.com

Top left
Beto Janz, photo by Raul Janz

Opposite
Broken Decks Skull

Broken Decks/SKULLS

Beto Janz customized used and broken decks to promote a new skate store in town, the "underground" way. Stickered with the store brand and address, they were left on the streets around Curitiba, Brazil – a gift for whoever found and claimed them.

©BetoJanz 2010

As seen in THRASHER MAG.

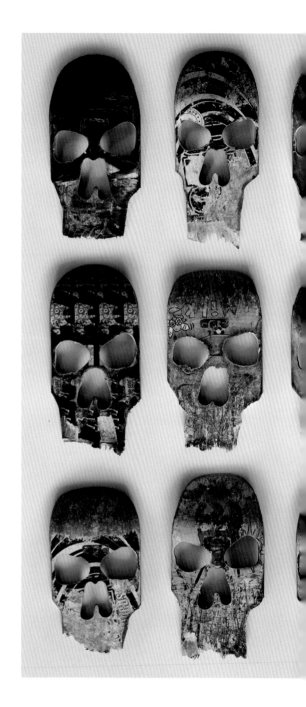

Broken Decks/SKULLS

Destruction/production process

BETO JANZ – FUCK OFF PROPAGANDA –

I WANT YOUR SKULL (1)

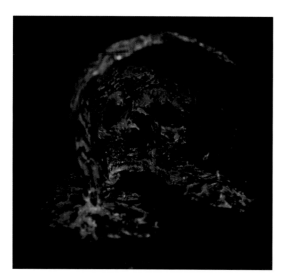

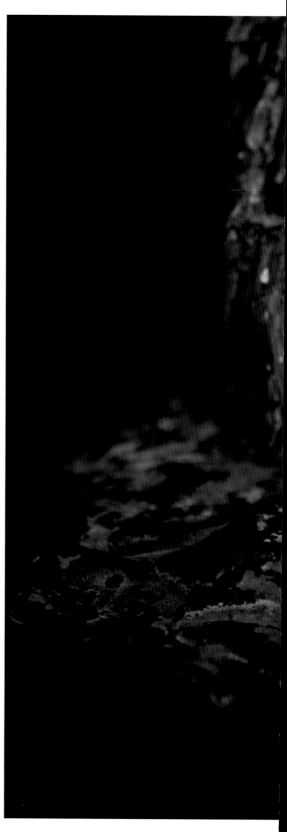

BETO JANZ

Hot Metal Bronze Skull

Bronze sculpture, 2013, © Beto Janz
With special thanks to FundiArt
http://www.fundi.art.br

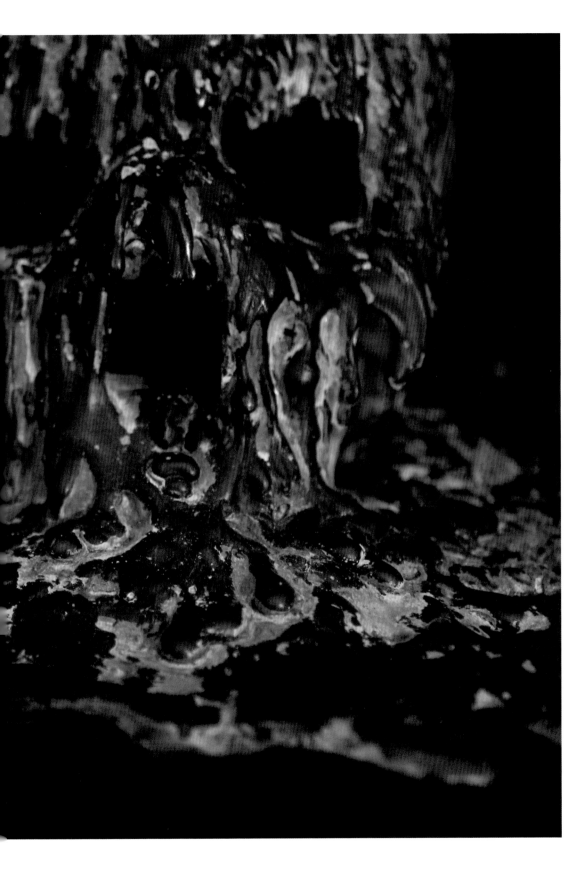

DEREK MAWUDOKU

Londoner Derek Mawudoku was born in 1959, graduating from Goldsmiths College of Art in 1987 with a BA (Hons) in Fine Art. His interests include drawing, comics, animation and printmaking.

"His powerfully expressive works are drawn directly from his own life experience ... he depicts the world as he finds it. The imagery is always raw and uncompromising ... intensely human" – Jon Thompson, from his Introduction to *Feed Me: The Monotypes of Derek Mawudoku*.

Derek's artworks have been acquired by The British Museum, private collections in the UK and USA, and are now shared here, with you.

http://www.prattcontemporaryart.co.uk

Opposite
Skull_001

Above
Skull_002

Opposite
Needle Time, dry point print

© Derek Mawudoku
www.derekmawudoku.co.uk

FRANCOIS ROBERT

Stop the Violence

Swiss-born, United States-based photographer Francois Robert may enjoy worldwide renown for his commercial work (Coca-Cola, BP, Western Union etc.), but he doesn't rest on his laurels. He also creates and exhibits Fine Art photography. Characteristically provocative in terms of its subject matter, his work ranges from Polaroid transfer prints to candid street and travel photographs, and still-life studies.

In his series Stop the Violence he rearranges real human bones to produce artworks unequivocally pointing up the tragic consequences of war. As he explains, "Conflict, aggression, suffering, and devastation . . . the human skeleton is often all that remains from such acts of violence. This is what you are left with after war – a body count. These images suggest an aftermath, therefore functioning as a warning."

www.francoisrobertphotography.com

Opposite
Stop the Violence –
Skull & Bones.
All work © Francois Robert

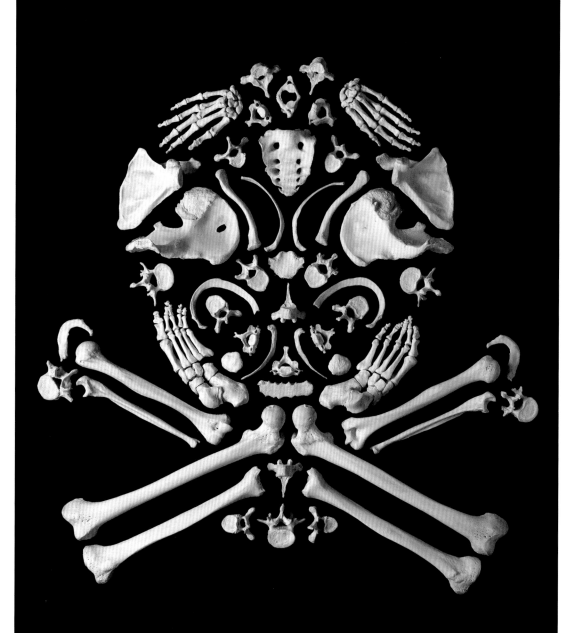

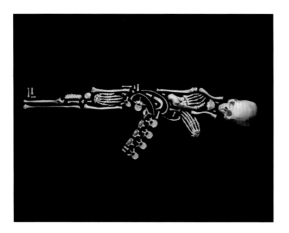

Above
Stop the Violence –
Kalashnikov

Oposite
Stop the Violence – *Tank*

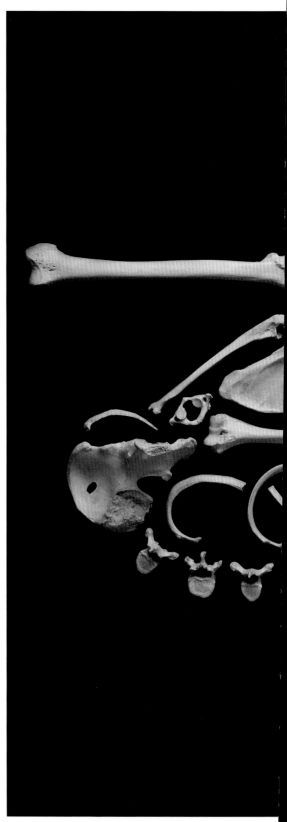

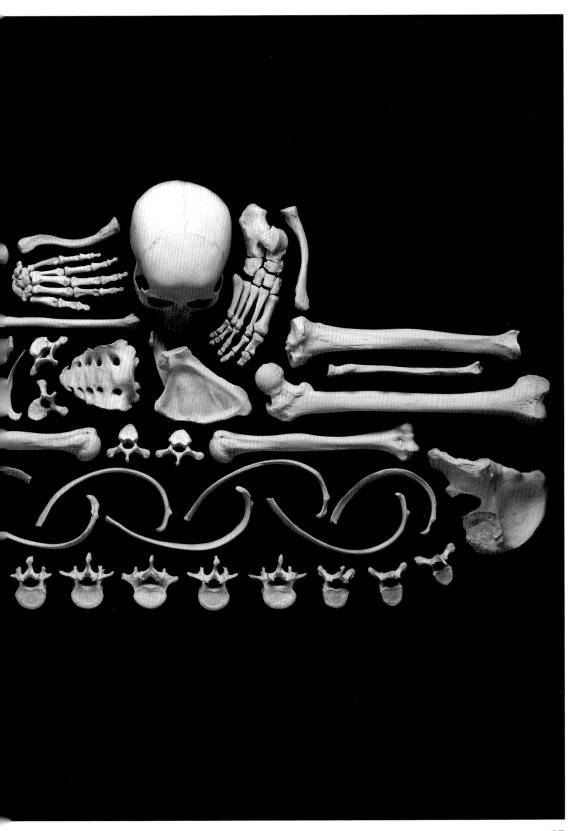

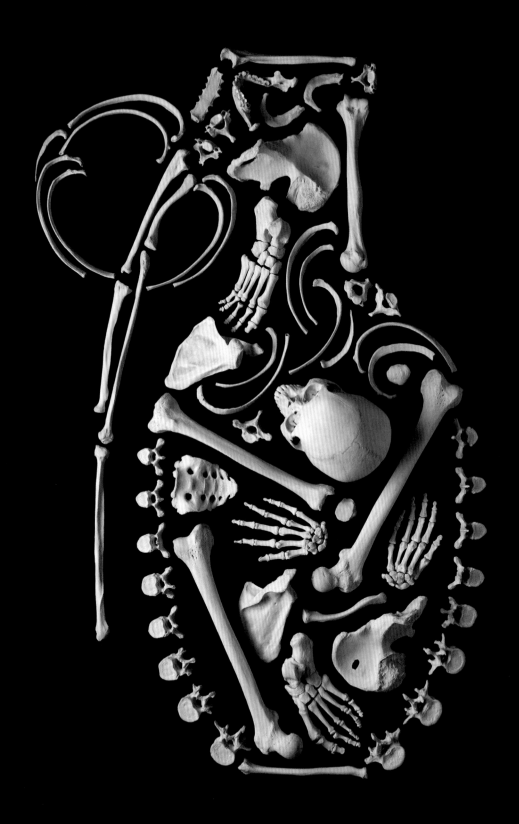

Opposite
Stop the Violence – *Grenade*
Above
Stop the Violence – *$*

Top
Stop the Violence – *War*

Bottom
Stop the Violence – *Oil*

Opposite
Stop the Violence – *Fighter Jet*

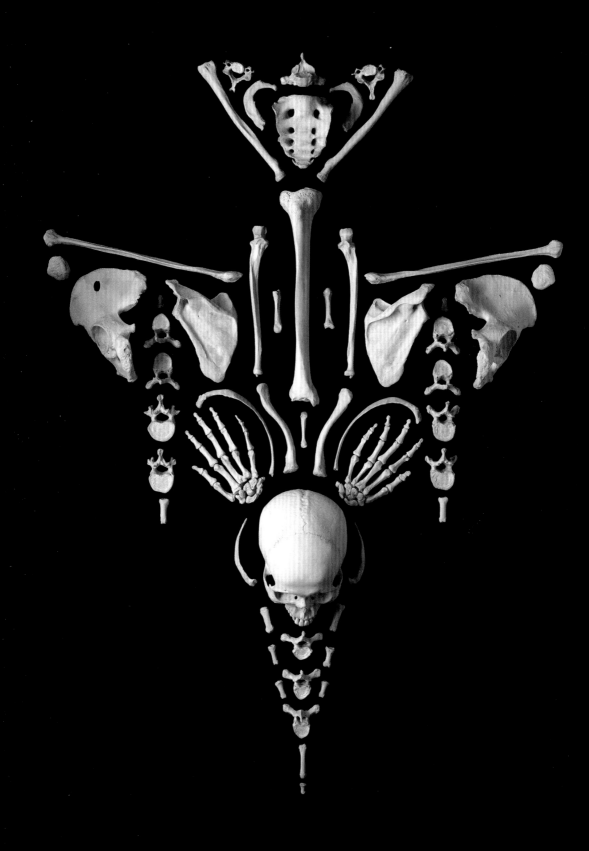

JASON MIDAS MITCHELL

Jason Mitchell has been drawing since he was in diapers.
He grew up going to punk rock and hardcore shows. This shaped
the topics in his art: race, drinking, trials of working-class life,
relationships, music and, of course, skulls. While he was attending
the Rhode Island School of Design, classmates would joke behind
his back, "Hi, I'm Jason Mitchell and I like to draw skulls."
Well, HA HA, he's now in this book, and they're not.

www.jsnmidas.tumblr.com

Top left
Skroulls (scrolls skulls) by
Jason MIDAS Mitchell

Opposite
The image of the plaid
painted canvas is made up
of four 16 x 20 in. canvases.
Clockwise from top left:
SKROULLdaggertongue2,
SKROULLone2,
SKROULLbootsy2
(as in Bootsy Collins, rapper
with the Furious Five, famous
for his starburst glasses),
SKROULLdemon2

After obtaining his Bachelor of Fine Arts in printmaking, Jason joined the URBAN FOLK ART collective and relocated to New York City. There he designed, printed and sold T-shirts for the collective, as well as NYC-based punk bands from the 90s till today; all the while "singing" for a few punk bands, including AS$TROLAND and MISCEGENATOR, playing shows at CBGB's, ABC NO RIO and others around the NY area.

In addition to his works with UFA, Jason prints and designs under the name MIDAS IMAGES, which stands for: Music Inspired Drawings Are Sound, or when self esteem fails: My Idiot Drawings Are Stupid.

Left and opposite
Scroll Skull Mirrors by Jason MIDAS Mitchell, 1/4 in. mirrored plexiglass, laser-cut and etched. Approximately 16 x 20 in.

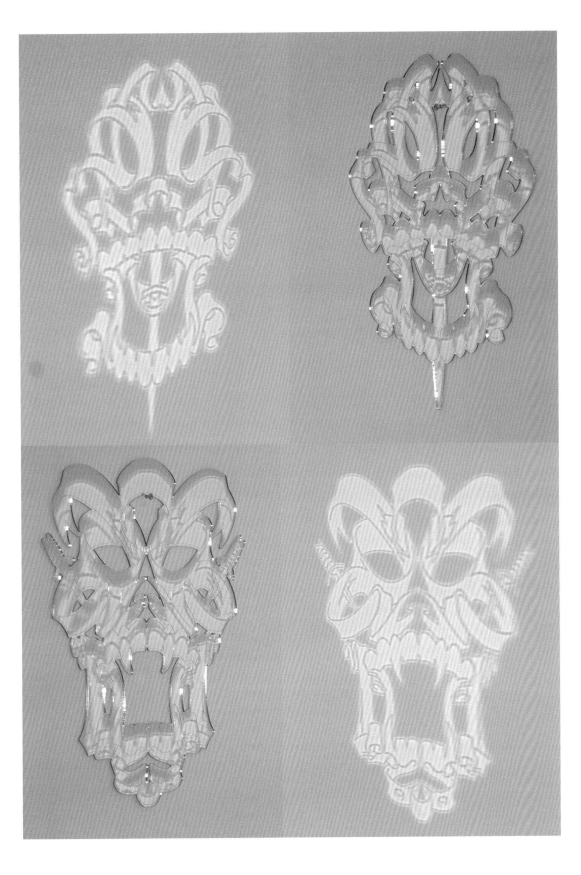

LINDA KING

Based in Hastings, UK, Linda King – called Inkylinda because of her many tattoos, mainly of her own drawings and designs – is almost unlimited in her mediums of expression as an artist: Painter, muralist, performance artist, prop maker and "Lily Gilder". She is, she says, of the "use what you've got/if it's not working stick more on/if it moves … decorate it/ if it doesn't … do same' school of magic-making.

Go and get your lilies gilded – "Exciting commissions considered with relish."

inkylinda@gmail.com

Top left
Written All Over My Face
Concept and Model:
Linda King
Head tattoo: Xed Le Head,
Divine Canvas, London
Photographer and Photoshop:
Adam Piggott
www.adampiggott.com
© 2009 Linda King and
Adam Piggott

Opposite
Voodoo Skulls
Plastic skulls from Poundland,
decorated with paint, feathers,
artificial flowers, dice and
toadstools
260 mm x 130 mm each
minus bases (inverted
earthenware flowerpots
spraypainted gold)
© Linda King 2007
Photographer:
Claire Richardson
www.clairerichardson.com

Skullibration
Oil on plywood,
594 mm x 677 mm
Photographer:
Claire Richardson
© Linda King 2007

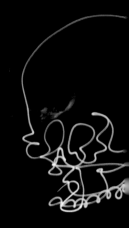

PETER CLINE

"Drawing and Photography are often seen as very separate disciplines. The former is unmistakably subjective, while the latter has a deceptive impression of objectivity. If you reduce the speed at which light enters the camera it reveals the creator's influence over the image, and their ability to make adjustments. With light painting, the photograph subtly captures the artist performing the drawing, and they too become part of the image. The momentary act of drawing in light lends itself sympathetically to the subject matter of the skull and mortality."
Graphic designer, Peter Cline

www.thethoughtpolice.co.uk
www.peterclinegraphicdesign.blogspot.co.uk

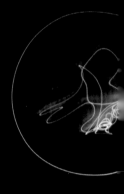

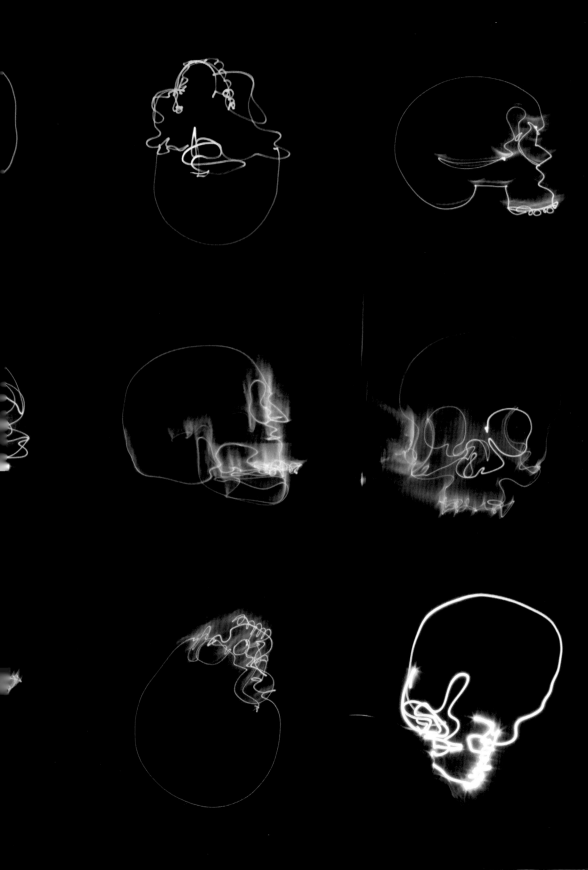

RANSOM & MITCHELL

Specializing in arcane illusions & impractical flights of fancy.

A still image and motion picture creative team based in San Francisco, Ransom & Mitchell combines the talents of director-photographer Jason Mitchell (not to be confused with Jason MIDAS Mitchell, elsewhere in this book) and set designer/photo illustrator Stacey Ransom.

Their in-depth process blog, Fake Believe, answers frequently asked questions, such as: "How'd you do that?"

A: "Our approach combines cinematic lighting with distinctive sets to create what cannot exist. (Defying the laws of gravity and logic . . .) We make the impossible practical."

www.ransommitchell.com

Behind the scenes – www.fakebelieve.net

RANSOM&
MITCHELL

Opposite
Portrait of the artist,
Charmaine Olivia

From "die Familie" – A series of Hysterical Reenactment Family Portraits – artist Dave Correia portrays Doktor Shreken Monstrum

Experiences in filmmaking nurtured Ransom & Mitchell's desire to be storytellers. Their heavily stylised imagery often has a strong narrative thread. "We custom build sets, props and use real-life FX." The resulting images are then manipulated in Photoshop, as many as 100 layers painstakingly stitched together.

Ransom & Mitchell draw great inspiration from Italian and
Dutch painters such as Caravaggio and Johannes Vermeer, using
chiaroscuro (light and shadow) to create imagery that subtly
blurs the lines between photographs and paintings.

"Begin doing what you want to do now. We are not living in eternity. We have only this moment, sparkling like a star in our hand – and melting like a snowflake."

Francis Bacon

Portrait of (co-creator) Jason Mitchell. (Look for the skull reflected in the windscreen.)

Right
Portrait of (powerhouse blog)
Boing Boing co-contributor
David Pescovitz
www.boingboing.net
Spot the skull in the jar,
as smoke, and another on
his jacket lapel.

Opposite
Ransom & Mitchell's self
portrait as *Orthros Sapien*.

"Everyone is an artist inside, and it's great that Instagram has encouraged people to just LOOK around them and share things they find interesting. We don't need endless money to chase our dreams, just resolve and time. Hopefully, we'll get to hang out on this earth long enough to escort all of our ideas to the other side."

Ransom & Mitchell, interviewed by Charlotte McManus

NOAH SCALIN

Crown Prince of Skulls

No matter where you look, no matter which way you might turn, there is no escape – American artist and designer Noah Scalin has you surrounded on all sides, especially when it comes to all things skull-related. In 2007 he initiated Skull-A-Day. Three hundred and sixty six skulls later (2008 was a leap year!), he had fulfilled his end of the bargain. Year Two was then turned over to viewer submissions …

Skull-A-Day is now in its seventh continuous year. Any way you slice it, that's a LOT of skulls! On the following pages, Noah shares with us just a few of his own.

www.alrdesign.com
www.skulladay.blogspot.co.uk
www.noahscalin.com

Top left
Pumpkin Anatomy, for Halloween 2010
(Check the website to see 2012's Bonus Skull no. 404: *Pumpkin Anatomy II*)

Above right
Noah Scalin – *Skeletube Package* (sale item)

Opposite
Skeletube V, customized vintage vacuum tube

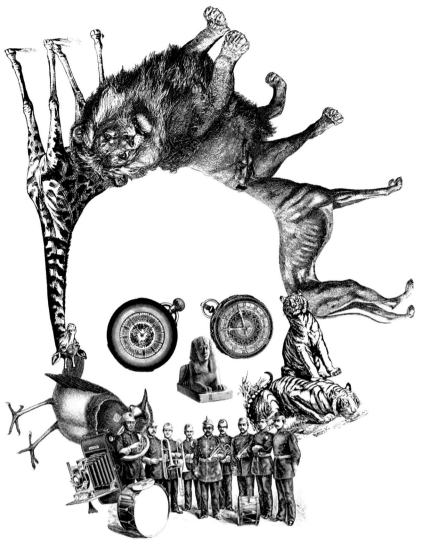

Opposite, top
Noah Scalin – *Skeletube
Army I*
Customized vintage vacuum
tubes

Opposite, bottom
Noah Scalin – *Tube 5 & 6*
Noah Scalin – *Tube 2 & 3*

Top
Noah Scalin – *The Menagerie
Skull*, arranged Victorian
illustrations.
Commission for Kenneth Cole,
www.kennethcole.com

Bottom
The Letterpress Skull was made
with the help of Purgatory Pie
Press, New York.
www.purgatorypiepress.com

Noah Scalin – *Dead Media*: anamorphic installation of 497 VHS videocassettes, 20 ft 8 in. x 8 ft 11 in. overall, commissioned by TCC (Tidewater Community College) Visual Arts Center in Virginia, USA.

In the spirit of the famous painting, *The Ambassadors*, by Hans Holbein the Younger, the skull was created anamorphically – it only becomes obvious from one fixed point of view and is actually quite distorted in real life.

These interventions in
the immediate landscape
call to mind the art of
Andy Goldsworthy, the
British sculptor, photographer
and environmentalist who
produces site-specific
sculpture and land art

situated in natural and
urban settings.

Opposite
Noah Scalin – *Mountain
Retreat Skull*: about 20 feet
long, made from leaves and
other natural materials,
on location.

Above
Noah Scalin – *Jumbo Snow
Skull*, a co-creation with
Paul Overton of Dude Craft,
www.dudecraft.com

"The installation took three days to complete – or rather nights, since I was coming in after hours to give the toxic fumes a chance to clear our before customers would arrive in the morning!"

Noah Scalin – *Skeleton Damask*, temporary mural installation in the Lamplighter Roasting Company's Loo Gallery (their actual bathroom), Richmond, Virginia. Each installation is painted over when the next artist creates their piece. The wallpaper is created with a damask-style (reversible figured fabric) pattern, using only the bones of the human skeleton. Two 18 x 24 in. stencils cut from thick, flexible mylar create one complete section.

Check out artist Noah, rocking his Bane/Punisher ventilation mask and skull-T.

June 4th, 2011 was the first official international Skull Appreciation Day. Inspired in turn by Strangely Orange Snack Appreciation Day (or S.O.S.A.D.) every June 21st, the folks at Skull-A-Day decided to start their own campaign – to have June 4th each year declared an official calendar celebration of cranial love! 2012's second international Skull Appreciation Day was celebrated with a one-day exhibition, held at Philadelphia's Mütter Museum, America's finest museum of medical history, www.collegeofphysicians.org/mutter-museum (an equivalent to London's superlative Hunterian Museum, www.rcseng.ac.uk/museums/hunterian based at the Royal College of Surgeons, and filled to the rafters with skullish curiosities, horrors and delights – for the strongest of stomachs only!) As well as auguring in Year 7 of Skull-A-Day, June 4th, 2013 and the third S.A.D was marked with an exhibition at the International Museum of Surgical Science in Chicago, Illinois, co-curated by Noah Scalin and Vanessa Ruiz of Street Anatomy. No greater love hath skull known!

This page
Noah Scalin – Skull Appreciation Day logo

Opposite
Skull Appreciation poster

JUNE 4

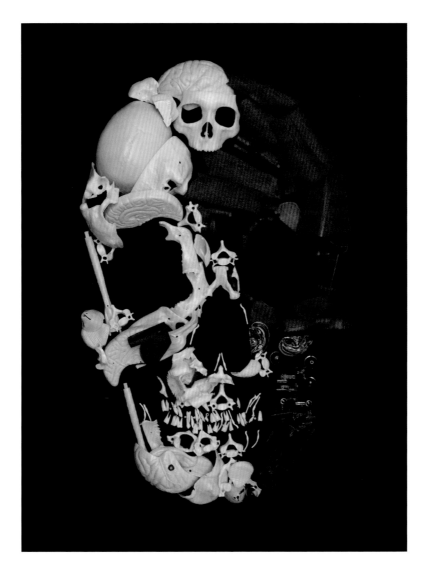

Above
Noah Scalin – *Visible Skull*:
made from the parts of a
vintage Renwal "The Visible
Head" model kit, circa 1960.
Opposite
Noah Scalin – *Safe Skull:
500 Arranged Condoms*

(approx. 22 x 16 in.)
#210 of Noah's original Skull-
A-Day project, in which he
created 365 skulls over the
course of a year, June
2007–08.

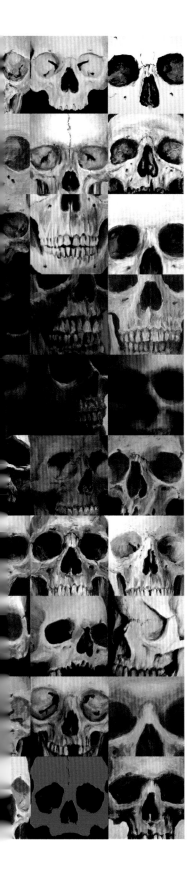

Noah Scalin's
100 Painted Skulls
Or 101, if you look carefully . . .
To celebrate year 5 of Skull-
A-Day, The Crown Prince of
Skulls, Noah Scalin decided to
paint 100 skulls on 4 x 4 in.
wooden panels over the
course of the year.
Available as an art print from
www.society6.com

www.alrdesign.com
Inspired by the enduring
legacy of punk rock activism
(and named with thumb
placed firmly on the nose)
Another Limited Rebellion,
Design Therapy & Creative
Consulting, was founded
by Noah Scalin in 2001 –an
effective business model for
the growing Corporate Social
Responsibility movement.
Also check out Noah Scalin's
books – *SKULLS*, featuring 150
images from the first half
of the Skull-A-Day project,
and *The Design Activist's
Handbook*, co-authored with
Michelle Taute – a practical
guide to making a living
while living by your ethical
principles.
www.skulladay.blogspot.co.uk
www.noahscalin.com

MIKE EGAN

Based in Pittsburgh, USA, artist Mike Egan has previously spent time working as an embalmer – which might just explain his fascination with skulls! His paintings are made using acrylic paint, shellac, wood and nails, telling compulsive stories about death, devils and saints.

"I'm greatly influenced by [the annual Mexican festival] the Day of the Dead, Halloween, horror films, churches, the German Expressionists . . . and my time in funeral homes," says Mike.

www.eganpaintings.com
www.yarddog.com

Top left
Death Came on Halloween,
Mike Egan
Acrylic and shellac on wood

Opposite
Every Time I Die I Think of You
Mike Egan

Clockwise from top left

Sharing My Colors

The Night I Got My Halo

Sharing My Blood With You

Night Watch

Remember Us When We Leave

Black Souls Gather

Mike Egan
Acrylic and shellac on wood

Top left
The Unlucky Bastard

Top right
*If I Die I'm Taking You All
with Me*

Bottom
The Zombies

Mike Egan
Acrylic and shellac on wood

EMPIRE DE LA MORT

Paul Koudounaris

Art historian (PhD in Art History, UCLA) and relic hunter
(a real-life Robert Langdon, from Dan Brown's *The Da Vinci Code*),
Paul Koudounaris is the author of international bestsellers *The
Empire of Death* (2011) and *Heavenly Bodies* (2013). In the first,
he explored charnel houses, ossuaries and reliquaries around
the world. For the second he gained unprecedented access to a
multitude of religious institutions (more than seventy, across four
continents) to rediscover ornamented skeletons, many of them
hidden away for over a century.

The Emperor of Death lives in Los Angeles, California, USA.

All photographs © Paul Koudounaris

Opposite

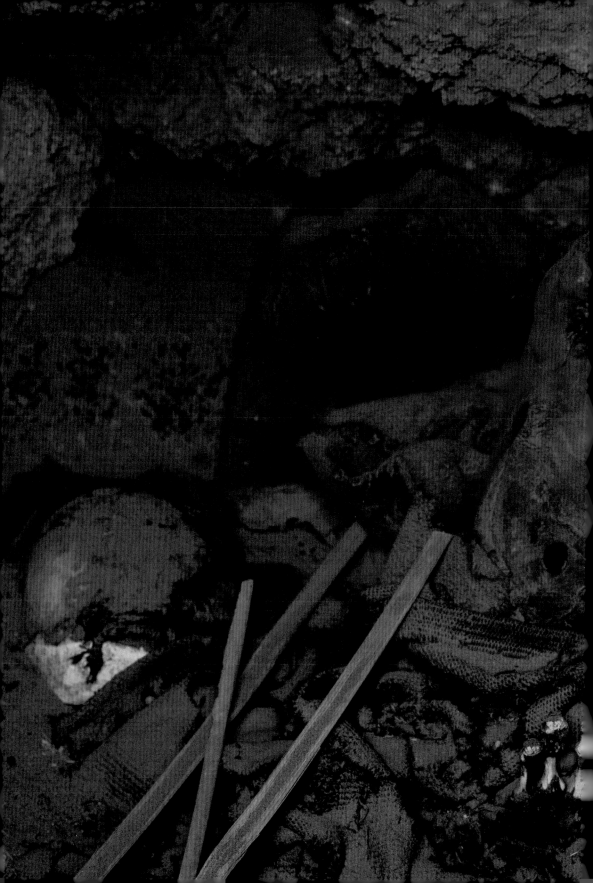

In 1578 a labyrinth of underground tombs were discovered beneath Rome, Italy – thought to house the remains of thousands of early Christian martyrs. These skeletons, known as "the catacomb saints", were distributed far and wide among Catholic churches and shrine sites – subsequently dressed, adorned with wigs, crowns, jewels and armour, and then posed in elaborate displays. They would act as reminders to the faithful of the treasures awaiting them after death.

In the intervening centuries, Western attitudes toward both the worship of holy relics and death itself changed sufficiently for these spectacular relics of purported saints to be hidden away, in many instances languishing almost entirely forgotten – waiting for the investigations of intrepid historian Paul Koudounaris to bring them once again to light.

Opposite
St Felix, Gars Am Inn, Germany

Following spreads
St Konstantius, Rorschach, Switzerland

St Valentin, Bad Schussenried, Germany

St Valerius, Weyarn, Germany

All photographs
© Paul Koudounaris

The largest skull festival in the world – bigger even than the Mexican holiday, Día de los Muertos – happens in Bolivia every November 8th: *Fiesta de las Ñatitas* – literally, "the little pug-nosed ones". Adherents believe that human skulls house the souls of the deceased, who act as protectors, helpers, and intermediaries for the living. Kept in shrines year round in the home, they communicate through dreams or visions in exchange for ritual offerings such as candles, coca leaves and cigarettes. Rather than commemorating the deceased, however they celebrate the power of the dead to affect the living. As Paul Koudounaris reminds us: "This is not . . . about the macabre or death. They are books about beauty and salvation".

All photographs © Paul Koudounaris

www.empiredelamort.com

Opposite
Ossuary (*Osario*),
Solferino, Italy
Remains from the Battle of Solferino in the Napoleonic Wars, with a connection to the founding of the International Red Cross.

Following spreads
Ossuary chapel (*Capela dos Ossos*), Alcantarilha, Portugal

"A tall grotto with Christ at the top of what looks like a layer cake made of bone".
Paul Koudounaris

Chapel of Skulls (*Kaplica Czaszek*), Czermna, Poland

Fiesta de las Ñatitas, Bolivia

DESIGNER SKULLS

Cool as a corpse, distressed, symbolic, simple or complex – the intervention of a smart graphic designer brings an edge to ever-present skull imagery that transforms it evermore into an example of indelible iconography. Logos, T-shirts, CD covers, tiles, posters, stickers, even metalware and chairs: the possibilities for product design that capitalises on a well-placed, expertly realized skull knows no bounds. Bow down before the skull. The skull rules above all!

Clockwise from top left
Paul Frank? No, Danny from UK comic *The Beano*'s Bash Street Kids, as created by Leo Baxendale. Homemade tribute sweater made by Smallbrainfield, on
www.flickr.com

Toy Figure X-Ray by BARDARON
www.etsy.com

Tippex on enlarged newsprint, design by ILYA

Opposite clockwise from top left
Souviens-toi-que-tu-vas-mourir (Remember that you will die), fiberglass chair memento mori by Pool
www.work.poolhouse.eu

Shirts for a Cure project T-shirt graphic by Mike Cavallaro
www.66thousandmilesper hour.com

Skull sample
Skull tape, Polemic Graphics '89

Skull Rasta by Jorge More
www.fb.com/ jorgemorecamisetas

104

Below
Risograph prints

Opposite
Compilation image from
a linocut book sequence,
showing a face being eaten
away by maggots to reveal
the skull underneath. Tasty!

www.ottopress.co.uk
www.thethoughtpolice.co.uk

PETER CLINE

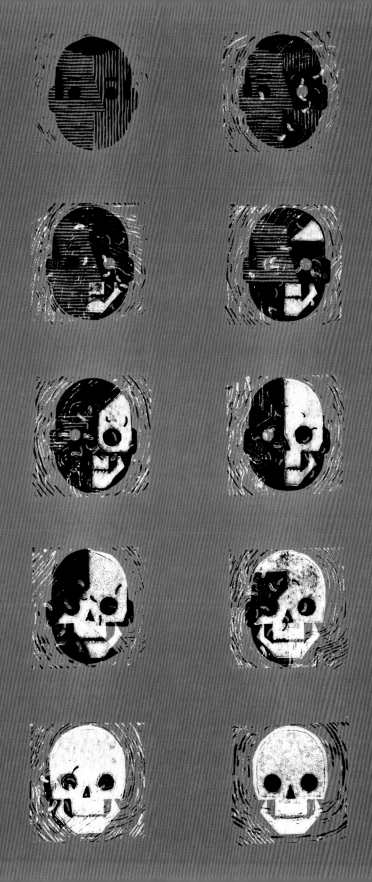

DEATH CIGARETTES

Hands up if you remember DEATH Cigarettes – a challenging brand sold by the Enlightened Tobacco Company in the UK from 1991 to 1999. Poised to make a comeback, apparently ... death never sleeps.

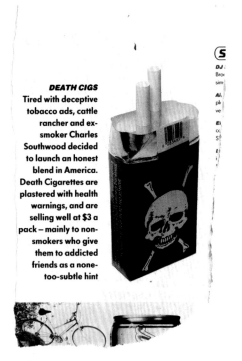

DEATH CIGS
Tired with deceptive tobacco ads, cattle rancher and ex-smoker Charles Southwood decided to launch an honest blend in America. Death Cigarettes are plastered with health warnings, and are selling well at $3 a pack – mainly to non-smokers who give them to addicted friends as a none-too-subtle hint

Top
Death cigarettes original packaging

Bottom
Clipping from style mag *The Face* (RIP)

Opposite
Imeus Design / Anthony Peters – *Happy Death*, cover design for *Viva* magazine, Issue 2, Brighton, UK.
www.imeusdesign.co.uk

Bottom left

Skullraisers – Jake – limited
edition print, bookplate design
for the graphic biography
HELLRAISERS
(Self Made Hero, 2012)
www.jake-art.com

Right

A Felicidade – Ricardo Castro
Illustrator, hobby philosopher
and frustrated artist Ricardo
shares a composition made up
of wood type around the word
happiness, in Portuguese.
www.diariodeumladrao.com

Opposite

MGP Madd Gear Pro logo –
shop window decal snapped
in Littleton, NH, USA.
www.maddgear.com

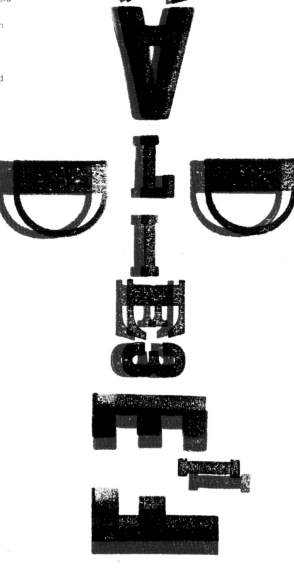

ALI GULEC

Is an illustrator and designer living in Istanbul, Turkey – the city that he cites as his main inspiration. Specializing in "popular urban artwork" he caters for laptop sleeves, smartphones, ereaders and tablet devices – but you could also decorate your bathroom with his large-scale vinyl stickers. Working via textile brand ikiiki design studio, which he founded in 2008, Ali loves to surprise with hidden messages and surreal conceptual creations, not least within his complex and intriguing T-shirt graphics.

www.ikiiki.co

Top left
Splash Skull

Opposite
From the Message series –
Skull 4

Above
Hometaping

Opposite
Geo Skull

Above
Humpty Dumpty

Opposite
Room Skull

All images © Ali Gulec

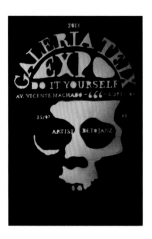

BETO JANZ

Top left
Stencil spray painted
exhibition poster, Cartaz Expo

All other pictures
Custom-Built Bike
Bicycle model CALOI 10/1985
(Fixed Gear) – custom
(100% handmade)
*"With thanks to my dad
(Raul W. Janz), for all the
support, help and knowledge
shared".* Beto

The cranium of a skull lends new life to even the most trivial piece of furniture: the chair. It is a direct reference to the designer's skateboard/rock'n'roll lifestyle. "One of the icons of this universe, the skull is an emblem of human limitation that remains after the end," says Beto.

Sadomasochism, bondage and corset piercing also feature. These elements are not intended to shock, however, insists artist and designer Beto Janz. "On the contrary, they give the piece an ambiguous delicacy."

www.betojanz.com

Chairs
4 Chairs, 2012,
Created for Desmobilia
www.desmobilia.com

BUSSOGA*

Surreal design

In 2010 Josep Motas, unable to find a production company willing to back his designs, started one of his own – joined in 2012 by the artist Irina Grosu. Their workshop is in Sant Jordi Desvalls, a small Spanish village nestled between the Pyrenees and the Costa Brava – the same wind-blasted landscape that inspired Salvador Dalí. Bussoga similarly strive for the surreal in something extravagant, weird, decontextualized, "to break the rules of physics and social behaviours".

www.bussoga.com

*Bussoga: is a word used in the Ampurdan
(north-eastern Spain) that means a bump from being hit,
usually on the head or forehead.

Most of Bussoga's products feature hand-silkscreened ceramic tiles. Made one by one, every tile is different – presenting characteristics that, in the past, were considered imperfections. Nowadays, when massive industrial producers make products that are identical, these handmade characteristics have become synonymous with character and quality.

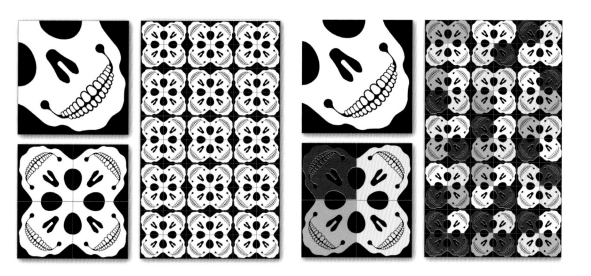

"The top goal would be for someone to like the tiles, retile their bathroom, then one day be sitting on the toilet and discover . . ."

Josep Motas

Skull

The initial idea for this design was to create a mosaic from geometric shapes, more or less pleasing to everyone – at first glance. On further inspection, the skull becomes apparent ... the aim, to shock a little: especially people who entertain stereotypes (i.e., that the skull = something bad).

"**Dead pop stars rotting in the studio**
Hear them on the radio
Dead dead dead dead dead"
"Dead Pop Stars" by Altered Images

DEAD FAMOUS

MJ, Cobain and Marley from the "Dead Famous Collection" by George Ioannou – who doesn't always limit his skullish icons to the deceased (he also does a mean David Bowie as Ziggy Stardust … to dust).

www.georgeioannou.com
www.artrebellion.co.uk

LUCKY NAKAZAWA

Los Angeles-based artist, printmaker and designer Kiyoshi Nakazawa periodically puts out one of the very best-looking zines you'll ever see (*Drunken Master*), containing one of the most exciting MMA (Mixed Martial Arts) comic strips that you could ever read. Graduating from the Art Center College of Design in Pasadena, California, with a BFA in Fine Arts, he's since worked for numerous publishers and clients including *Mattel*, *LA Weekly*, *Dark Horse Comics*, *World War III Illustrated*, *Giant Robot* magazine, *Destroy All Music*, *Thrash Out* and many more. Do yourself a favour: grab hold for a great time!

www.luckynakazawa.com

Above
Lucky Naka Elvis Frank

Opposite
Cover from *Drunken Master*

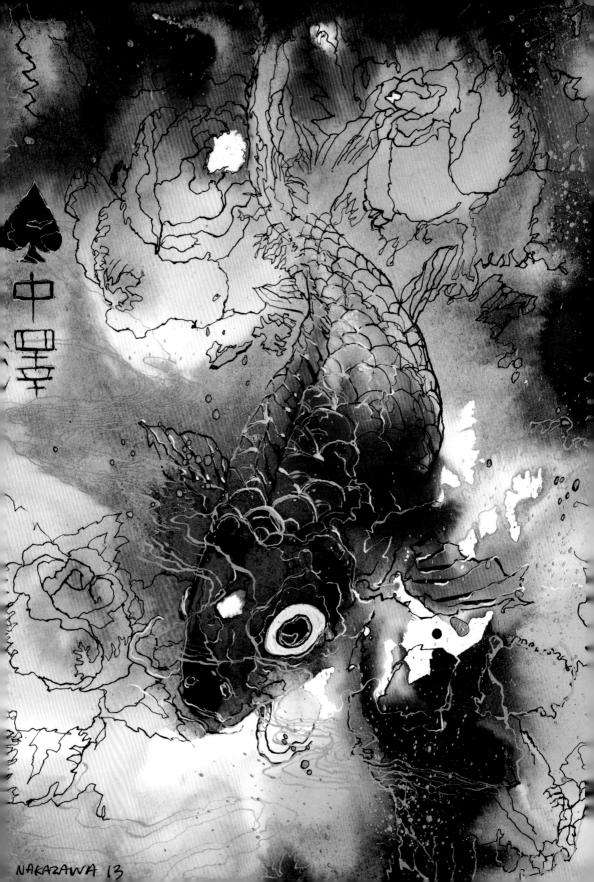

NAKAZAWA 13

Opposite
Koi, Roses, Skull. Watercolour
and ink on watercolour paper.
Private commission

Above
Water Skull. Watercolour and
ink on watercolour paper.
Personal work

Above and opposite
Illustrations from *Drunken Master*

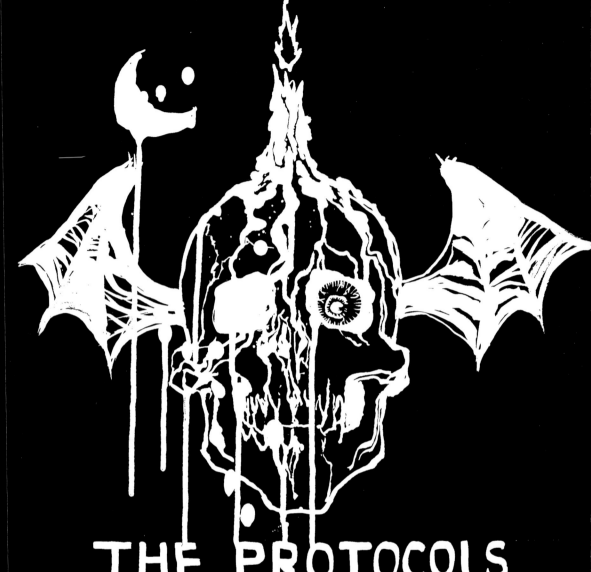

THE PROTOCOLS

OF THE

ELDERS OF ZION

Opposite
Protocols of the Elders of Zion 2. Brush and ink on paper. Originally done for the art show *The History of Conspiracy*

Above left
Rumble Flesh. Silk screen. Originally done for *Greasers, Ghouls and Gals* art show

Above right
Huntsman. Silk screen on paper. Personal work

METHANE STUDIOS

Mark McDevitt and Robert Lee

Both hailing from small midwestern towns, Robert and Mark bonded over bad 80s haircuts, corndogs, good music and creating art, while they majored in Illustration at Columbus College of Art and Design, Ohio. In 1998, their enduring friendship spawned Methane, a two man studio creating package designs, logos, and silk-screened posters for the East Atlanta music scene. Among others they dig David Stone Martin, Jasper Johns, Ralph Bakshi, Mort Drucker, Robert Rauschenberg, Warhol and Edward Ruscha. "We use the computer like a pencil or paint brush, but we still belly up to the drafting table often. Our goal was always to tell a story, convey a message . . . make someone stop and think a little with our designs."

www.methanestudios.com

Top left
Steer Stripes

Top right
Heavy Trash

Opposite
Peace Skull

Following spread
The Dead Weather Bride
and *The Dead Weather Groom*

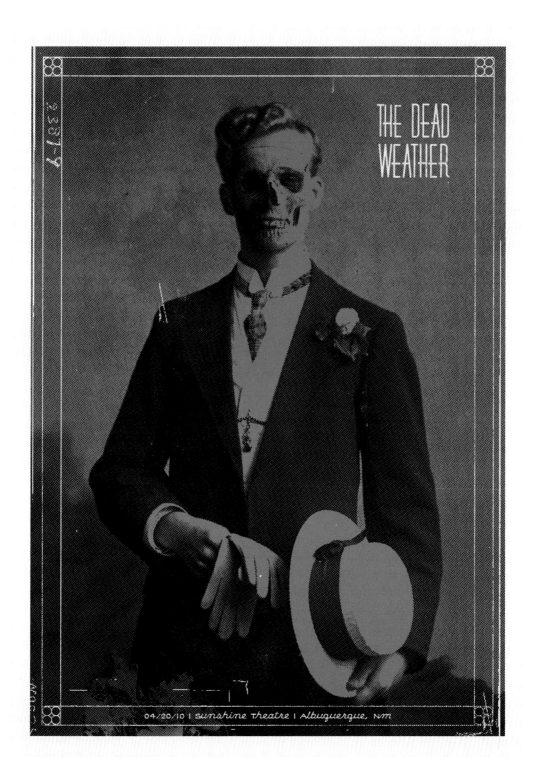

THE DEAD WEATHER

04/20/10 | Sunshine Theatre | Albuquerque, NM

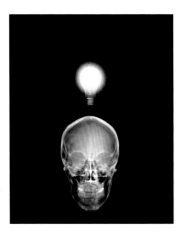

RIAN HUGHES

Designer, typographer and illustrator Rian studied at the UK's London College of Printing before a brief round of advertising, music industry and style magazine duties. He's worked extensively for the British and American comic industries, including both DC and Marvel – if you follow *Captain America*, *Wolverine*, the *X-Men*, *The Spirit*, *The Invisibles* and many more, you have probably already been admiring one of his logos. He recently collaborated with ex-Spice Girl Geri Halliwell on a series of six children's books, and releases sexy new fonts via his own designer label.

He has an extensive collection of *Thunderbirds* memorabilia, a fridge full of vodka, and a stack of easy listening albums which he plays very quietly.

www.devicefonts.co.uk

Top left
Skull new.tif

Above right
Ray Death for *Death Ray* magazine (Mascot), 2007

Opposite
From *Soho Dives, Soho Divas* book, by Rian Hughes, 2013, Image. Collaged life drawing and photo of warning sign on electrical substation taken in northern Italy

Below
Deadline "Dead Head"
mascot illustrations, *Deadline*
magazine, UK, 1993

Bottom
X-ray Kid – Gaming company
logo design, 2010

**Opposite, clockwise
from top left**
X-ray Kid – Gaming company
logo designs, 2010

Sect Civil War – logo designs
for a Valiant Comics crossover,
2013

"One of the most successful and prolific designer/illustrators of the past 20 years"

Roger Sabin, *Eye* magazine

Above
Pirate music logo and
skull logo

Opposite
Skull logo

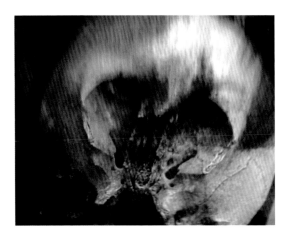

DESIGNER DEATH

Through a lens

Design guru Rian Hughes is also a keen photographer (see his report from Rome in the Skullpture section). Here he reports back from the front lines of death with a deft collection of signage featuring skulls and other manifestations – proceed at your own peril.

All photos © Rian Hughes

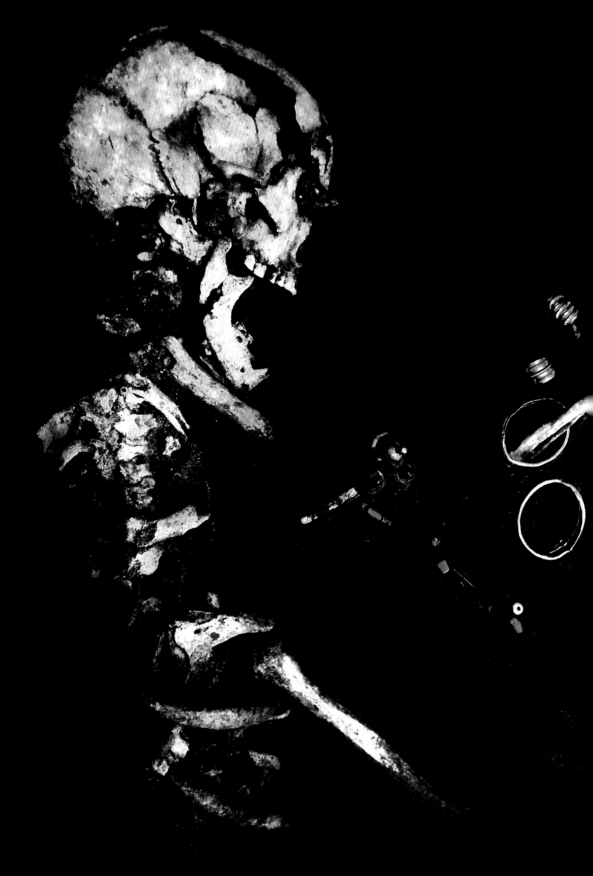

Top
Danger signs, Oman

Bottom
Defence du Mort, France, 2006

Opposite
Skull sign , Morocco, 2008

"Old Inca
skulls,
hundreds
of years old.
The tombs lie
just beneath
the surface,
and people rob
them, leaving
the bones
propped up
around."

Nazca, Peru, 1994

SKELETON KNIVES

John Thrower

These are the joys of the unusual, the thrill of the unexpected.
First, in form – a skull design more akin to that of a mask, be
it African-influenced tribal motif or a gas mask, or even the
disturbing distortions of a deep-space alien. Then, in seeing those
same skull designs in the context of the mundane and everyday –
as toothpicks, a lanyard. Sometimes these simple yet deep and
complex joys may be found in the sheer, compelling beauty of the
image – a tiny skull bead delicately balanced on the keen blade of
a knife. Maestro metalworker and designer John Thrower trades
in all of these, and more . . .

www.skeletonknives.com

All photographs and designs © 2013, John Thrower

Top
Skull bead balanced on a
stainless steel Frosts blade
from Sweden, the handle
machined aluminum,
anodized black.

Opposite
Dios de Muertos Bronze Skull
(the skull balanced on the
knife blade)

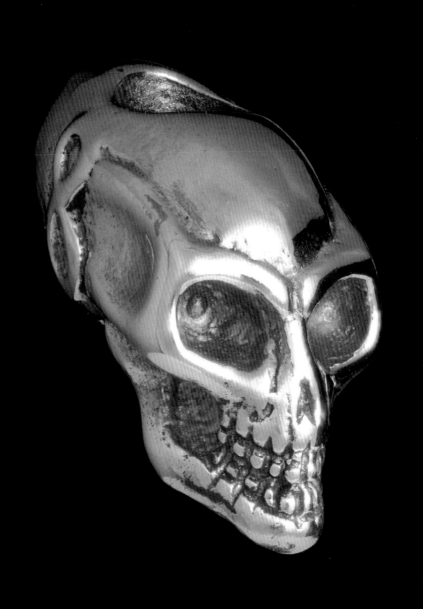

Opposite
Infinity Skull, bronze
"The *Infinity Skull* represents
the vastness of space and the
many alien life forms that
may be out there."

This page
Alien Skull Bronze Bead,
polished finish

This spread
Dios De Muertos Bronze Skull,
and Bronze skull as a lanyard

"This skull has watched over the passing of lives from this life to the next as an ancient skull atop a funeral staff."

Design inspiration taken from India

ILLUSTRATED SKULLS

Whether rendered in delicate pencil or swathes of pure black Indian ink, strokes of the nib or plotted digital pixels, skull imagery continues to inspire and excite illustrators the world over.

Magazine illustration, book covers, games design, personal projects, warm-ups and sketch sessions, and just plain ol' doodles – for publication, for projection, for fun. Here is just the briefest sampling of what's recently been on the drawing boards of some very talented folks indeed.

Bottom left
Cover design to unknown Finnish paperback, from Skullfinder General Soren Mosdal
www.sm.anport.dk

Opposite, clockwise from top left
1986 thrash metal T-shirt design
www.voivod.com

Halloween Greek Style, poster artwork by Vasilis Lolos for Hearts and Swords tattoo Studio
www.steamrobo.blogspot.co.uk

Awe Skull by Zven Balslev
www.cultpump.blogspot.co.uk

Mxckxy Death, post-it note phone pad doodle by editor ILYA, in reference to his latest graphic novel, *Room for Love*
www.selfmadehero.com

Didn't you ever notice how a skull brings to mind the helmet of an Imperial Stormtrooper? Plate VII, old engraving by William Miller resampled for a Burke and Hare graphic novel, 2011. Image courtesy of Rian Hughes

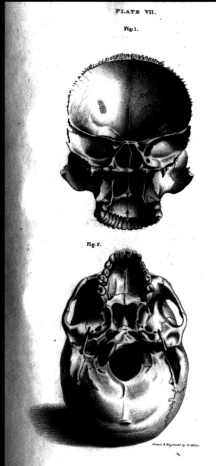

Ortheza
The Way to the Witch

Ortheza is the pen name of
Lukasz Matuszek, from Poland.
A concept artist for games
(character and equipment

design) and an illustrator
of book covers, his work has
been featured in *ImagineFX*
and *Pixel Arts* magazine.

www.ortheza.net
www.ortheza.deviantart.com

Opposite
Jerzy H. Szostek

The skull-ish cover to
cartoonist Jerzy's self-
published stripzine, *Human
Soup*, Issue 5, almost akin to
an African mask.

www.poopsheetfoundation.
com

Right
Gary Leach
Jeff Jones tribute

American artist Jeffrey
Catherine Jones (1944–2011)
was best known for comics
and book covers, in addition
to Fine Art. World-renowned
fantasy artist Frank Frazetta
called Jones "the greatest
living painter" – high praise
indeed, if you know of
Frazetta's work. Although
Jones first achieved fame as
Jeff Jones and lived for a time
as a man, she later changed
her name and was legally
recognised as female.

www.web.archive.org/
web/20110908023201/http://
www.jeffreyjones-art.com

Gary Leach is most famous
for his work with Alan Moore
on the revival of Marvelman,
Miracleman.

"I was talking to a lady, late thirties, in my street, and she was wearing a black top with a huge and glittery silver-coloured skull on her chest. She got a mild ribbing over it naturally. Danny of the Bash Street Kids can get away with it without bother, teens just about manage it on occasion. Mister and Missus Older look a little bit desperate for attention."

Jerzy H. Szostek, Liverpool

Shari Hes
Exorcist

Shari Chankhamma is a comics artist, illustrator, colourist, reluctant writer and technology enthusiast from Thailand (see *The Mammoth Book of Best New Manga*, Volumes 1–3). She sometimes goes by the name of Shari Hes.

www.sharii.com

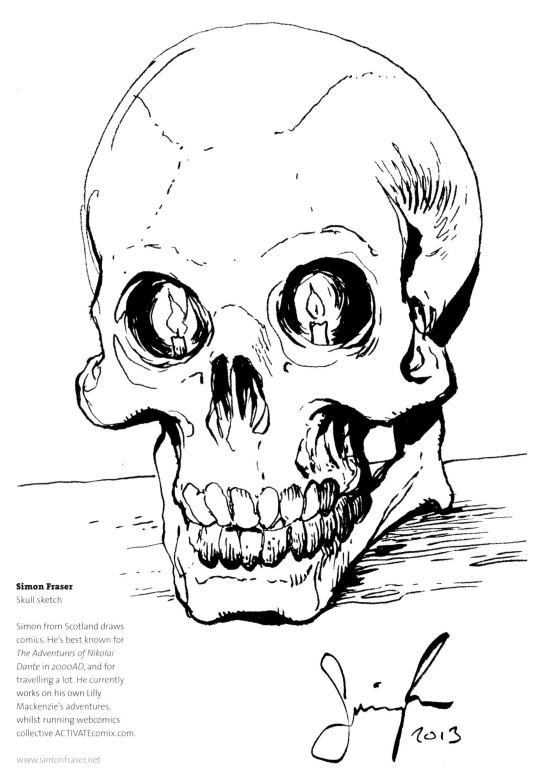

Simon Fraser
Skull sketch

Simon from Scotland draws comics. He's best known for *The Adventures of Nikolai Dante* in *2000AD*, and for travelling a lot. He currently works on his own Lilly Mackenzie's adventures, whilst running webcomics collective ACTIVATEcomix.com.

www.simonfraser.net

Karen Rubins
Skullspider

Subtle post-Victorian Goth
Karen Rubins is a comics
creator and illustrator living
and working in London.
In 2009 she was official
Comics Artist in Residence
at the Victoria and Albert
Museum, London.

www.karenrubins.com

Jose Muñoz
Skull sketch from Kendal
Lakes Festival, 2013

Born in Buenos Aires,
Argentina, Jose was
understudy to both Alberto
Breccia and Hugo Pratt, two
mighty giants of comic art.
Very much an "artists' artist",
he nowadays commands
huge respect himself, and
joins them in the pantheon
of legend.

www.josemunozdessins.com

Opposite
Jon B. Cooke
Tekeli-li! Journal of Terror, No.1,
from 1991 © Jon B. Cooke, 2013
Illustration © Bob Eggleton,
2013

www.jonbcooke.com

A MONTILLA PUBLICATION

NO. 1, SPRING 1991

Tekeli-li!

J O U R N A L   O F   T E R R O R

PREMIERE ISSUE!

SPECIAL
LES DANIELS
NUMBER

featuring
Don Sebastian
the Vampire in
"The Dead Man"
with an Interview,
Bibliography,
Appreciations,
& Critical Essay

Plus:
Chet Williamson
Bob Booth
Robert M. Price
Bob Eggleton
Stefan Dziemianowicz
James Thompson
Allen Koszowski
Steven Gould
John Borkowski
and much more!

$4.50

Opposite
From *Ocular Anecdotes* by designer Peter Cline, an example of vector graphics.

www.ottopress.co.uk
www.thethoughtpolice.co.uk

Above
Hot Skull Action featuring Kid Savage, by Ben10 co-creator Joe Kelly and ILYA, for Man of Action Studios ©2013 Kelly/ILYA – an exciting new comics character soon to make his debut. Watch for it!

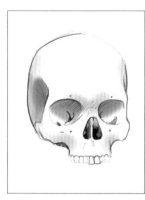 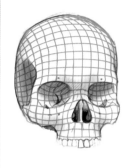  

BARRY THOMSON

An illustrator and animator based in Glasgow, Scotland, Barry Thomson has a keen interest in painting traditionally and digitally, as well as creating and drawing his own short comic strips. Self taught, he follows in his father's footsteps as a professional illustrator. He is always striving to improve, whether by drawing in his sketchbook, or attending life-drawing sessions.

www.thomsonvthomson.com

Honey Skull
Step-by-step-process
(top, left to right)

Digital illustrations and text © Barry Thomson

Process 1
Firstly I drew out a rough of a human skull. I wanted to capture the front and the depth of the eye sockets and nasal aperture. This would give me more challenging contours.

Process 2
I then divided the skull into a flowing grid, as this would help keep a uniform size to the hexagonal honeycomb pattern.

Process 3
The stepped tiling of the hexagonal combs would be the most challenging part of the illustration by far. The grid's vertical and horizontal lines have to be used purely as a rough guide, but a guide nonetheless.

Process 4
Originally, I wanted to depict honey, and give myself the challenge of creating a translucent viscous liquid. But, in the end, I spent more time creating a skull out of the comb. The bees were then added one by one, leg by leg, hair by hair, onto the finished skull.

Opposite
Honey Skull,
digital illustration
© Barry Thomson

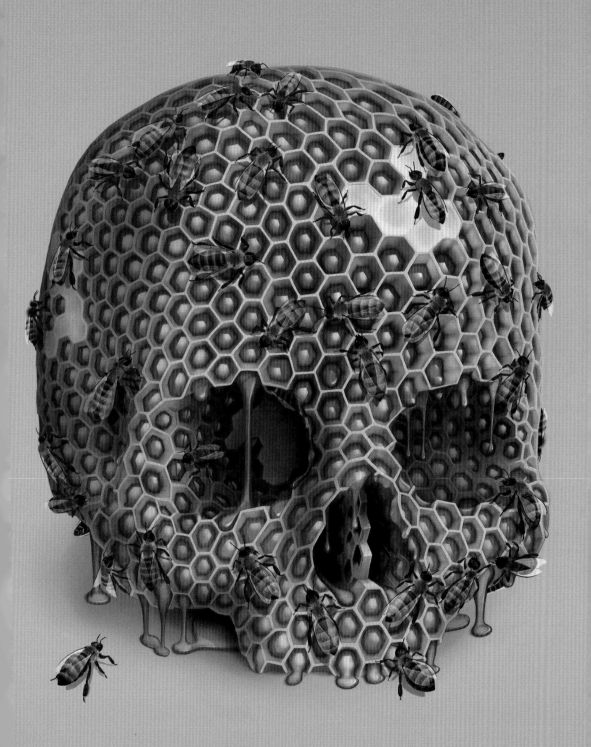

CHIE KUTSUWADA

A veteran appearing in two volumes of *The Mammoth Book of Best New Manga*, Chie Kutsuwada was born and brought up in Japan. After graduating from the UK's Royal College of Art, she now lives and works in London as a professional *mangaka* (writer and artist of manga, the Japanese form of comic strips). She attends manga-related events worldwide, and runs manga workshops for schools, libraries, and museums across the UK, including the British Library and the Victoria and Albert Museum. She adapted *As You Like It*, for the Manga Shakespeare series published by SelfMadeHero, and *Hagakure* (with Sean Michael Wilson) for Kodansha.

www.chitan-garden.blogspot.com

Kiss of Death,
digital drawing, skull yaoi kiss
with lilies and ivy.
Sketch (above) and final
illustration (opposite).
© Chie Kutsuwada, 2013

DONYA TODD

Her Tumblr page reads, "Donya makes comics about foulmouthed girls, French boys + fried chicken", and you can't really say better than that. Donya Todd – illustrator, painter and comic artist – lives on a remote farm near Newquay, in Cornwall, England. She takes her inspiration from the magical, marvellous and macabre. And rightly so: according to an Egyptian dentist that she once met, "Donya" means "the World" – and to any German, her surname sounds like "Death". Hence, "The World of Death"!

As if that weren't daunting enough, she is also the editor of badass girl-comic anthology, *Bimba*. Donya's debut graphic novel *Death & the Girls: Foul-Mouthed Adventure Through a Psychedelic Wonderland* is available now.

www.donyatodd.co.uk
donyatodd.blogspot.com

Top left
Hotdog Mu – *Death & The Girls* © Donya Todd 2013

Opposite
Death & The Girls
© Donya Todd 2013

Above and opposite
Poster to co-launch Donya's
Death & the Girls at London's
premier comics emporium,
Gosh!

www.goshlondon.com

MARK STAFFORD

Mark Stafford, "cartoonist to the stars, court jester to the functionally illiterate, and drain on the nation's resources", remains a largely undiscovered genius. He's been quietly ploughing his very particular furrow for many years, and is only now beginning to come to the wider world's attention. It's not right, I tell you! Check the website for a selection of his paintings, comic strips, and illustrations, then remember to wipe your feet.

Mark Stafford recently adapted Victor Hugo's novel *The Man Who Laughs* (a vital antecedent to Batman's Joker) with writer-chum David Hine. Cartoonist-in-residence at London's Cartoon Museum since 2006, he's also painted a mural for the graphic novel section of the John Harvard Library, close to Borough tube station. Worth a look!

www.hocus-baloney.com

Above
Mexicana Posada

Opposite
And Lo! There was a Fifth Rider, and his name was light entertainment, and Hell followed with him.
(In reference to the biblical Four Horsemen of the Apocalypse – War, Famine, Conquest and ... uhhh, The Other One.)

Top
Sketchbook skulls

Bottom
Mexicana Posada II

Opposite top
War and Peace

Opposite bottom
Li'l Death in Joyland

Kriminal – from the people that brought you *Satanik*! Inspired by *Diabolik*! Ik, ik, ik! Kreated for Italian comics in 1964 by Magnus and Max Bunker, and featuring the exploits of English master thief, Anthony Logan, dogged by death despite his canny skeletal disguise.
Kriminal © Editoriale Corno.

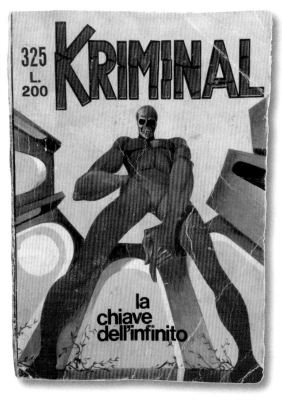

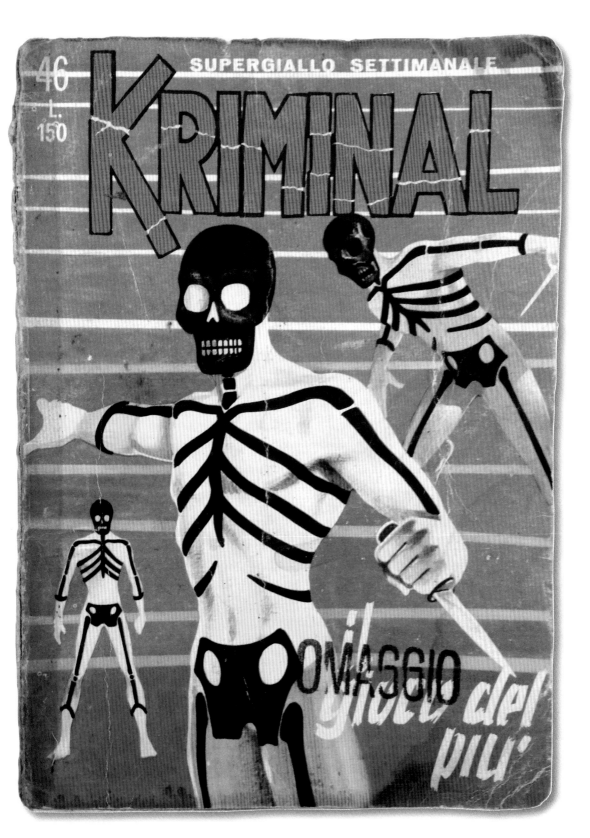

NICK SHEEHY

Nick Sheehy is an Australian-born artist and illustrator living in the south-east of England. After studying bronze sculpture in the wilds of Tasmania, Nick gave up on art, only to re-discover his love of drawing whilst living in London, sparked by an interest in the city's low-brow art, illustration, street art and graffiti. In his work, Nick explores the dreamlike, sometimes semi-autobiographical scenes and oddball characters that echo from his childhood imagination.

Employing a laborious technique, building up layers of texture and thin colour, his work infuses precision and attention to detail with random abstraction and clumsiness. He enjoys drawing various weird things for himself, exhibitions, publications and occasionally the odd client.

"Drawing loads of skulls [is something] which I haven't fully indulged in since I was a teenager, listening to Carcass, Sepultura and Pantera," says Nick.

www.showchicken.com

www.instagram.com/showchicken

188

Above
The Damage

Opposite
The Woodcutter

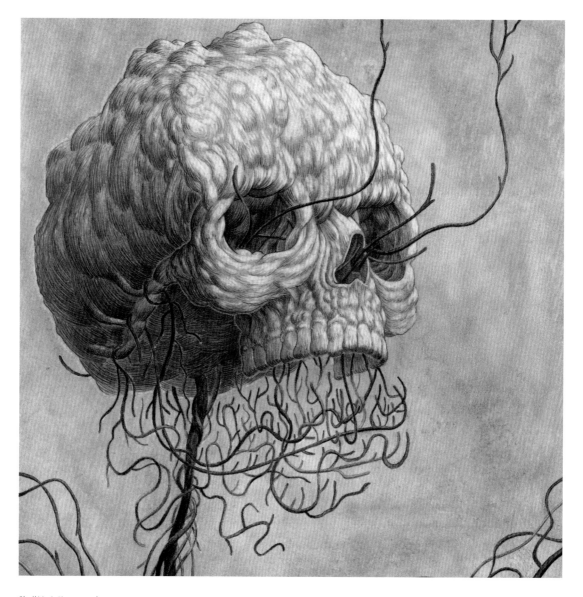

Skull Variations 1 and 2

All images © Nick Sheehy

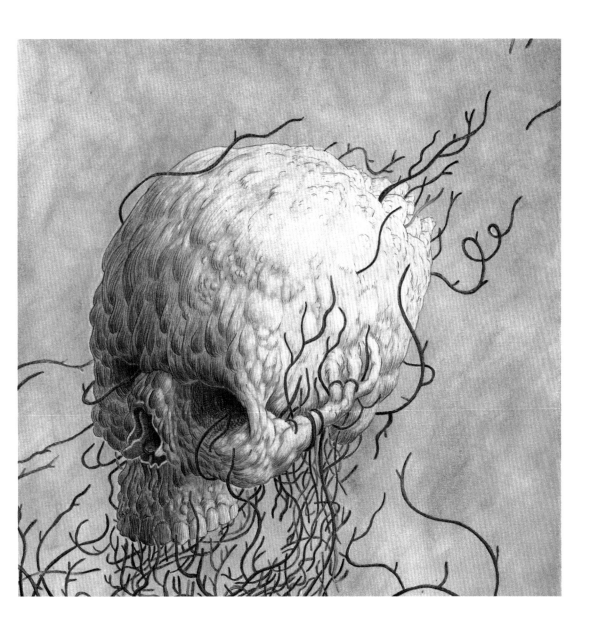

PETER JARVIS

Studied animation at the University of Creative Arts, Farnham, before making Toronto, in Canada, and the rainforests of Costa Rica – where he developed his passion for nature – his home. Back in England, he now paints and sculpts in Newport, Essex, where he owns a gallery. Peter is also a tattoo artist, and runs a mobile disco!

www.eight-infinity.com

Top, left to right
His Candy, East Meets West
Peace Skull, Her Candy

Opposite top
Peace Skull

Opposite bottom
Romance Skull

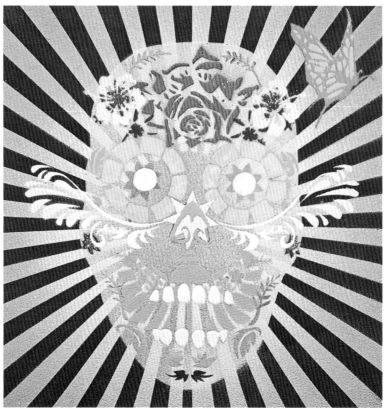

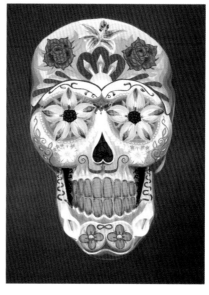

Sugar Souls, Peter Jarvis

Inspired by Mexico's Day of
the Dead (*Día de los Muertos*),
these skull paintings ascribe
soul elements to various
lifestyles.

Opposite
Sea Soul

Clockwise, from top left
Bird Soul
Mexican Soul
Lucky Soul

Acrylic on canvas, 24 x 30 in.

TOMMI MUSTURI

Artists, designers and illustrators don't come any more prolific or generous than this particular gent from the frozen north, Finland's Tommi Musturi. Tommi likes to draw – often in live performance – and since 2005 or so has concentrated on comics. He also translates "decent comics" into Finnish and distributes books and records through his Boing Being label. As a kid, he was an army-base brat. Following 10 years living in the capital city, Helsinki, he nowadays eats, sleeps and loves in Tampere, working with the KUTI KUTI collective (comic art studio & association). His websites arc laser bolts to the eye. Rock on, Tommi of Finland!

"We aim to do it all by ourselves, dig it hand-made. Freedom is . . . pretty much a war against all the plain dead stupidity that surrounds us. Dig what we do or not, most likely we'll keep doing this stuff until the end." KUTI KUTI

www.tommimusturi.com
www.boingbeing.com
www.kutikuti.com

Above
Mantta

Opposite
Big Beat, (sketchbook series)

Following spread
Sketchbooks

Opposite

From *Beating*, gathering images from 2003–2013, mostly from sold out fanzines and picture books: 128 pages, 200 images, "one big mess".

Below

Pixeled with a joystick on Commodore 64, colour adjusted some twenty years later for *Death to Most*, a pamphlet of Tommi's teenage drawings.

Following spreads

Cover image to *Specter*, an oversized (A3), 40-page anthology from KUTI KUTI on a Horror and Science Fiction theme, "a reality show indeed". Says Tommi, "I tried out (poor man's airbrush) blow pens for the first time, which, in spite of fainting, was kind of fun."

Sketchbook series, Tommi Musturi

Miss Universum, zombie portrait of some year's candidates

apparel noir

SKULL FASHION

Ah, fickle fashion – from Alexander McQueen's innovative designs on the catwalk, via Ralph Lauren's rugby-polo nexus of faux-classy casual thuggery, down to street market stalls and Third World sweatshops, like a rash.

It's in! It's out! It's hot! It's not! Skulls can now be found on almost any fashion product you care to mention – Catherine Rapetti clutch bags, Barker Black Skull Wing Tip brogues, Paul Smith cufflinks.* We'd feature them here but they're all far too expensive, and the aspirational lifestyle is just so yesterday. As a passing fad Skull Fashion has surely exhausted itself. But when all is said and done, sighed at and discarded, you can be sure of one familiar face-without-a-face that will still be sticking around – and smiling. For those truly in the know, there lurks a deeper trend that never goes away.

*all to be found in a handy round-up at

http://dustyburrito.blogspot.co.uk/2009/10/skulls.html

Thank you, Dusty. You've been there so we don't have to.

Top left
Death Kitty, apparel noir – designer label logo from the UK's Petticoat Lane

Above
Black tiny skull necklace, vintage-inspired acrylic jewellery. "Wear with this season's 'Goth Luxe' trend, with lace, black leather or a simple, white buttoned-up shirt."
www.maggieangus.com

Clockwise, from top left

Fireman Sam (yes!) Valentine
sports an unofficial
Fire Service sweatshirt,
snapped drinking at a bar
in Manchester, NH.
Photo: Robin A. Boylston

Diabolik pewter skull pendant
rocker necklace
www.tattoodonkey.com

Skully silk scarves modelled
by Anon Exhibitor at Comica
Comiket, and skulls collector
extraordinaire, Rebecca
Snotflower.

Previous spread

Goth to go to and *Spawn*
writer David Hine unzips
Guess top to model his
Gama Go T.

Above and opposite

David Hine, writer of *Poison
Candy* for Tokyopop, shows
off more of his Skull Tees
collection – including Shiroi
Neko, as not liked at all by
urbandictionary.com

If you can keep your skull tees on, when all about you
are losing theirs, yours is the Earth and everything that's in it.
And – which is more – you'll be a Man my son!

Above
Bulletproof Coffin co-creator
(with artist Shaky Kane),
David Hine models Parasuco,
Italian style.

Opposite
Alex shows fidelity to Linkin Park

A THOUSAND SUNS ✈ WORLD TOUR 2010

Skinny(ish) Goth rocks Fat Punk, Yoyogi style.

David Hine, sick puppy behind
Avatar's *Crossed* series, and *FVZA:
The Federal Vampire and Zombie
Agency* for Radical Comics,
absolutely swears 100% by his
very favourite fashion label:
Australia's purveyors for Surf 'n'
Street, Mambo Design.

Above
Mambo strikes twice with this killer Hawaiian design. Model: man about town David Shenton, who supplies us with his own bespoke cartoon anecdote concerning said shirt.
www.dscomics.co.uk

Opposite
Skull shirt by Denim is Everything. Photo: Chie Kutsuwada

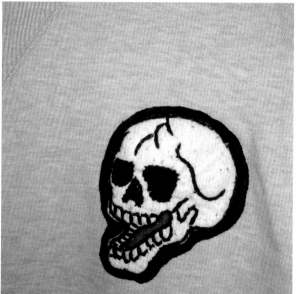

Top and opposite
Cowichan sweater by
Canadian brand Kanata.
"I bought it at the casual
men's clothing section at
Liberty. It was very expensive for me as a student, but it was
love at first sight so I couldn't
resist." Chie K

Bottom
Skull pullover by Pink Dragon

Top
Skull top, Brave Soul, UK.
Photo © Vyla Rollins

Bottom and opposite
Gold tooth skull hoodie,
Chie Kutsuwada, 20 ANS of
The Duffer of St George
www.thedufferofstgeorge.
com

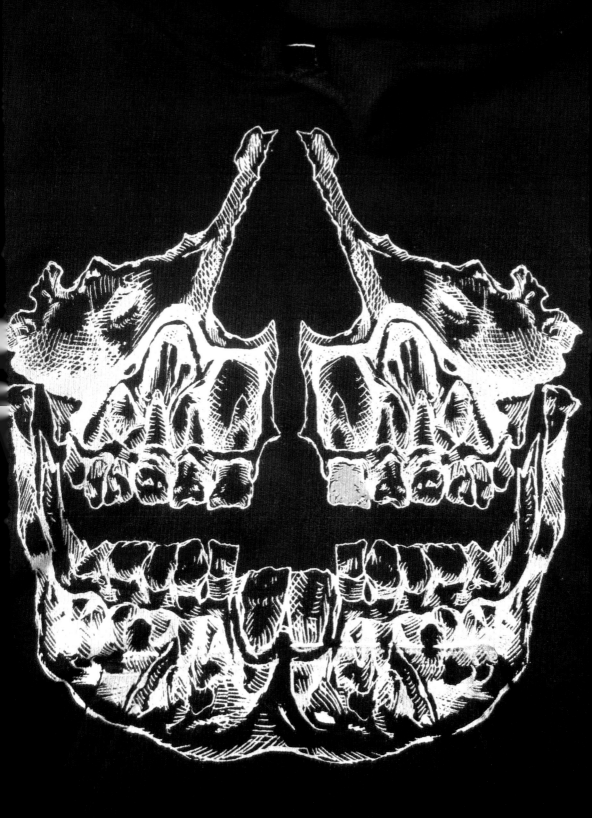

Belt buckles and bags: leathers from Lewes, UK, where pirate fashions, civil war couture and vaudevillian voodoo yet holds sway, and local Bonfire Societies in outrageous costume gather to mark the Glorious Fifth (of November: Guy Fawkes night). Photos © Vyla. Death or Glory!

Bottom

Skull buckle shoes from 1980s' London, via Germany: from the collection of Veronika Streitwieser. These survivors from the earliest days of post-Punk fashion and the likes of Kensington Market are worth digging up for the Eighties revival! Tschüss!

Right and opposite

The original adverts from a Bogey's Underground Fashion from London catalogue ("Superklamotten für Teds, Popper, Punks, Mods . . ."), featuring these very same boots. You too can dress like your heroes, Adam Ant and Bow Wow Wow, glam pirate-highwaymen. Ridicule is nothing to be scared of!

BOGEY'S

512

513

513

BOY

514

JEWELLERY

Skull rings have ever been a favourite fashion item, most especially amongst the alternative, hard rock rebel, Sons (and daughters!) of Anarchy and death metal set. Just one never seems enough! Magic man and comics cultural guru Alan Moore always sports a brace of them, and thus, so do many of his fans and followers – even when poised to rifle through a longbox of tattered back issues.

Left
Photo © Andy Bleck.

Opposite
Skull by T-Dog Junior
(see following spreads)

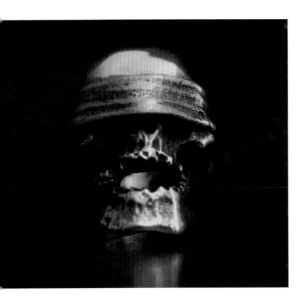

T-DOG JUNIOR — DOG STATE

Established in London, in 2004, Dog State was founded by designer and jeweller Takahashi Toshi (T-Dog Junior). Valuing the importance of traditional techniques, he specializes in modern skull and animal designs handcrafted to the highest standard, through his manipulation of precious metals.

www.dog-state.com

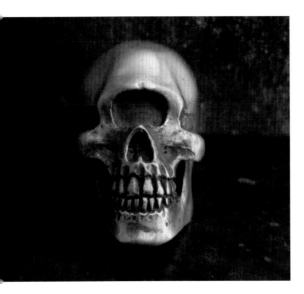

Top
Blindfold skull ring

Bottom
Cyclops skull ring

Opposite, clockwise from top left
Dokuro

One-eyed skull

Skull bangle

Skeleton key pendant

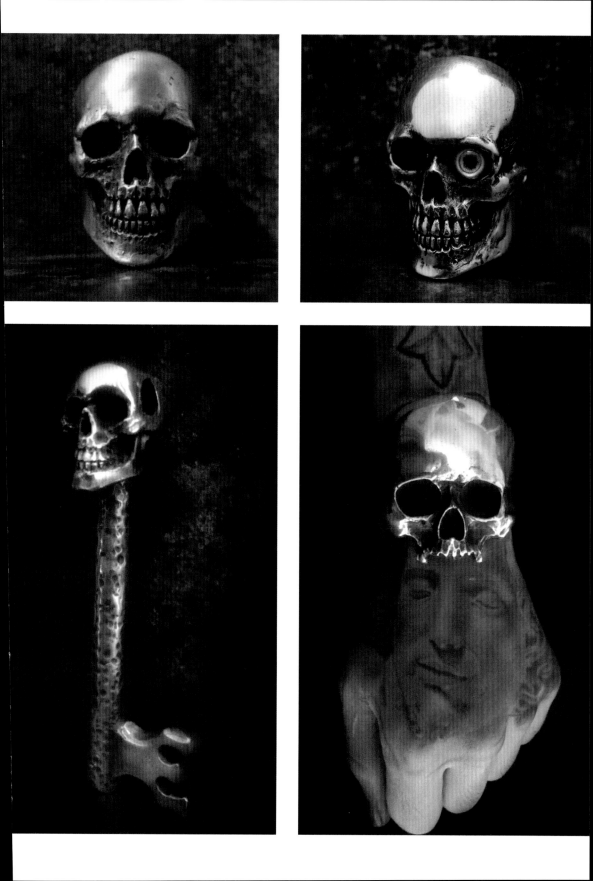

Bottom left
Indian skull ring

Bottom right
Tibetan Kapala skull ring

Opposite
Bunny skull ring

Following spread
Snail skull ring, Mandala skull ring

All images © Takahashi Toshi
(T-Dog Junior)

 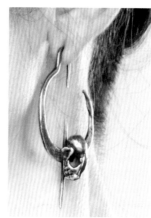

MIYU DECAY

Stephanie Inagaki

Ending this Skull Fashion section on the highest possible note, we present Miyu Decay (Me, You, Decay?), based in Los Angeles, California, USA. Crafting a careful selection from her favourite materials (sterling silver, carnelian, bone, feathers, vintage kimono fabrics) Stephanie Inagaki melds modern macabre with Old World grace and finery.

www.stephanieinagaki.com
www.miyudecay.etsy.com

Top left
Brass skull and cross bones keychain

Top right and opposite
Sterling silver gauged crescent bat hoop earrings and Tuareg palmier necklace

Photography: Allan Amato
www.allanamato.com
MUA: Jill Fogel
wwwjillfogel.com
Model: Ashley Joy Beck
www.ashleyjoybeck.com
Styling: Stephanie Inagaki
www.stephanieinagaki.com

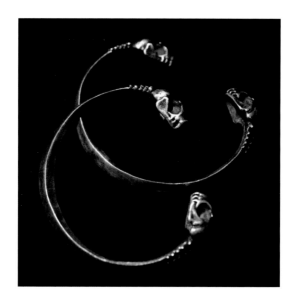

Top to bottom
Sterling silver bat skull
bracelet, necklace and
cufflinks

Opposite
Sterling silver bat skeleton
necklace

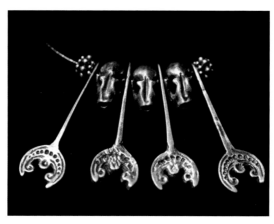

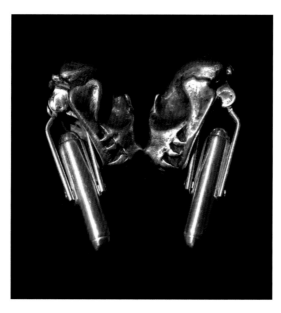

Sterling silver bat skeleton
necklace.
Solid sterling silver, hand cast,
made out of hand-forged and
filed sterling silver wire.
It took over 2 years to produce.

Photographer: Aaron Hawks
www.http://aaronhawks.net
MUA: Jill Fogel
www.jillfogel.com
Styling: Stephanie Inagaki
www.stephanieinagaki.com

CARTOON CUTE SKULLS

Nothing defuses fear quite like ridicule. From the Bergman-riffing dinner party scene in Monty Python's *The Meaning of Life* (Part VII – Death) to the Darwin Awards, we like to laugh ourselves silly in the face of death. The certainty of our own mortality makes us want to seize hold of the so-called Grim Reaper, with his flesh-stripped perma-grin, and to make him the bony butt of our own stupid jokes – or else ourselves the perennial butt of his. And what better way to reclaim control than to make eternity's icon of death iddle-widdle wiv cutesy puffy cheeks? Awwwww.

Clockwise from top left
Skull Hatter, Timur Hassan
timhassanart.tumblr.com

Skeletor, arch enemy of
He-Man, from the Masters
of the Universe Filmation
cartoon based on the toy-line
by Mattel. (See also right, in
colouring book and cosplay
versions.)

Comic Skull and Cross Bones
www.neatoshop.com
JollyRogersSkull,
vector artwork,
www.all-free-download.com

Deathshead Danny Morgan's
immortal sweatshirt design
from the Bash Street Kids,
reproduced as a sticker

Opposite, clockwise from top left
Tiny Skull Knight © Roberto
Garcia Garza
www.skyraptor.deviantart.com

Marks & Spencer glow-in-the-dark stickers, giveaway with
sweets, Halloween 2013

Skeletor on his skull throne
www.bustatoons.blogspot.co.uk

Skeletor and He-Man

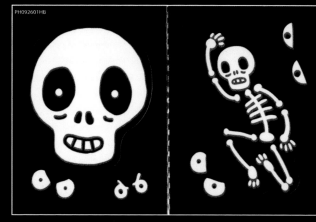

PH092601HB

Death's-head Kappa,
Craig Conlan

"The Kappa is a creature from Japanese mythology – a river-dwelling creature which tips boats over and eats you, by sucking your innards out through your anus. Nice! It has a turtle's shell and a pool of water in its head. You can defeat a Kappa by bowing to it. It will have to bow back and the water will tip out of its head, leaving it powerless. Thwarted by good manners, I love that!" – Craig

"Coffins stood round, like open presses,
   That shaw'd the dead in their last dresses;
   And by some devilish cantraip slight,
   Each in its cauld hand held a light."

To be read in a Scottish accent (if you're not sure,
rent Austin Powers or something . . .)

Above
Tamoshanter Skell, Craig
Conlan

A panel excerpt from *Gran
O'Shanter*, Craig's mini-comic
re-telling of "Tam O'Shanter",
the famous epic poem by
Robert (Rabbie) Burn

Opposite
Malady in her You Only
Live Once T-shirt

Internet slang and popular
hashtag, YOLO is the modern
equivalent of *Carpe Diem*
(Kill the Fish*) or a *Memento
Mori* – implying that it's best

to enjoy life while you have it.
Malady is a Conlan original –
of which there are many.
(*actually, Seize the Day)

All images © Craig Conlan
craigscomicland.blogspot.com

SKULL GAGS OLD AND NEW
Some jokes just never get old.

Top
Found magazine clipping of
an old cartoon, circa 1980s,
signed: dinden

Bottom and opposite
Veteran cartoonist Howard
Cruse shares with us, from
the vaults, Potty Jokes (the
1969 original) – and then,
through the miracle-power of
his stippling pen, resurrects it!
(Potty Jokes, 2013)

www.howardcruse.com

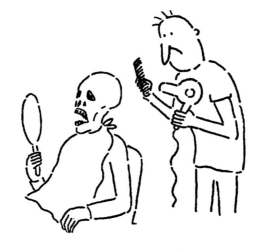

*"When I said I wanted the Elvis look I
meant from when he was still alive."*

Clockwise from top

Death Comes a-Calling,
Woodrow Phoenix,
ink on Post-it note
www.woodrowphoenix.co.uk

Skully 4, *Sketch Skull*, and
Skully 2, Mark Stafford
www.hocus-baloney.com

The monstrously talented
James Harvey/Harvey James
killer combo – zine cover,
Summer 2008
harveyjames.tumblr.com

Top
Monkeys vs Skeletons print,
Jonathan Edwards
www.jonathan-e.com

Bottom left
9 of Spades, Erica Smith.
Erica has designed a blazin' card
deck with Skulls as one of the
suits – as they should be! Get
out of here with your namby-
pamby diamonds and hearts.
www.wordsmithdesign.co.uk

Bottom right
Louche Skell, Jonathan Edwards
www.jonathan-e.com

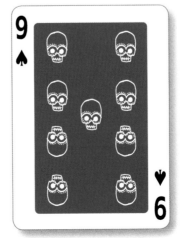

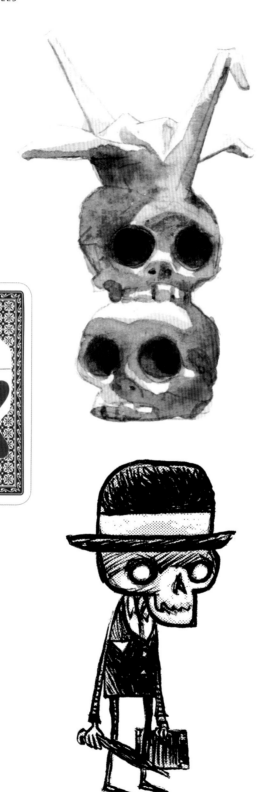

Clockwise, from top right
Anniversary, Glyn Dillon

Skully 3, Mark Satafford

Jim 8 Rosetti Plus, Zeel –
skull card
www.zeel.co.uk

Opposite
Xolo, from *B+F*, Gregory (Gory)
Benton, his new wordless
fable published by Adhouse
Books
www.gregorybenton.com

8/20

©2013 GREGORY BENTON

Top to bottom
Skeleton Roundels, Zeel
(Geoffrey Coupland)

foetusskullbugs1, Zeel
(Geoffrey Coupland)

Some skullies, Zeel (Geoffrey
Coupland)

Opposite
Skulls, Michiru Morikawa.
The work of this fabulous
illustrator can be found in
volume one of *The Mammoth
Book of Best New Manga*
(2006). Living in Japan, she
works as an art teacher in
junior high school.
Find her on Facebook.

Top to bottom
Pollockry skull,
Zeel (Geoffrey Coupland)

Primer for site,
Zeel (Geoffrey Coupland)

Fumanskull,
Zeel (Geoffrey Coupland)

Opposite
*You're Never Alone on a Desert
Island*, Justin "Scrappers"
Morrison

www.scrapperstown.com

Right
Do fear the reaper,
Zeel (Geoffrey Coupland)

Opposite
Stencil skull,
Zeel (Geoffrey Coupland)

www.hocus-baloney.com

REAL-LIFE SUPERHEROES

Something of a phenomenon, as reflected in an incisive and moving HBO documentary, the Real-Life Superheroes movement counts more than a few skull-bearers amongst its ranks: Death's Head Moth; Phantom Zero; Thanatos (Ancient Greek personification of Death). Inspired by their love of comic books, these guys actually patrol the streets dressed like this – more often helping out the homeless and such, than to discourage the real-life bad guys. And that makes them larger than life good guys. Chew on that, KickAss!

www.reallifesuperheroes.com

Top, left to right
Phantom Zero, Ghost and Thanatos

Opposite
Death's Head Moth
All photos by and
© Peter Tangen, except
Ghost (by Anon)

STREET ART SKULLS

As with every other type of artist, skulls hold curious sway over those who treat the blank white wall and brick expanse as their gallery or arena of expression. Scrawled in ink and paint, collage, stickered or sculpted, skulls hold sway – a reminder perhaps of their piratical / outlaw affiliation and cachet for those who choose to craft their art at the very outskirts of legality.

Top left
Random find (sticker)
Photo: ILYA

Top right
Punk stamp, Miqui One Stop
www.facebook.com/MiquiArt

Bottom
Buff Bars, Dan Holliday
www.danholliday.com
"The home of Punk Rock
Printing"

**Opposite, clockwise
from top left**
Streets of London, photo ILYA.
Throw-up Skull
by Justin Morrison
www.scrapperstown.com
Streets of Paris, Attendez,
Cross Now. Death Foxes
Youth, photo ILYA. Streets
of Rome, photo Rian Hughes

ATTENDEZ
LE SIGNAL
POUR TRAVERSER

FOXES YOUTH

AZIONE

LLA FUGA I PIONIE

Bottom, left and right
WELCOME TO FEAR CITY
Scaremongering (anti-) tourist
leaflet, New York, 1970s. NYC
Council for Public Safety.
Alarmist admonitions
included "Avoid public
transportation", "Conceal
property in automobiles",
"Do not leave valuables in
your hotel room, and do not
deposit them in the hotel
vault". In other words, PANIC
and RUN!
(Thank you to Woodrow
Phoenix for the welcome)

Opposite
DEATH FOXES YOUTH (Vanitas)
Ironic juxtaposition of
flyposters – Commercial Road,
East London, UK.
Photo © ILYA, 2013

WELCOME TO FEAR CITY

A Survival Guide for Visitors to the City of New York

WELCOME TO FEAR CITY
A Survival Guide for Visitors to the City of New York

The incidence of crime and violence in New York City is shockingly high, and is getting worse every day. During the four month period ended Apr. 30, 1975, robberies were up 21%; aggravated assault was up 15%; larceny was up 22%; and burglary was up 19%.

Now, to "solve" his budget problems, Mayor Beame is going to discharge substantial numbers of firefighters and law enforcement officers of all kinds. By the time you read this, the number of public safety personnel available to protect residents and visitors may already have been still further reduced. Under those circumstances, the best advice we can give you is this: Until things change, stay away from New York City if you possibly can.

Nevertheless, some New Yorkers do manage to survive and even to keep their property intact. The following guidelines have been prepared by a council of firefighters and law officers to help you enjoy your visit to the City of New York in comfort and safety.

Good luck.

1. **Stay off the streets after 6 P.M.** Even in midtown Manhattan, muggings and occasional murders are on the increase during the early evening hours. Do not be misled by the late sunsets during the summer season. If you walk in midtown at about 7:30 P.M., you will observe that the streets are nearly deserted.

2. **Do not walk.** If you must leave your hotel after 6 P.M., try not to go out alone. Summon a radio taxi by telephone, or ask the hotel doorman to call a taxi while you remain in the hotel lobby. Follow the same procedure when leaving the restaurant, theatre, or other location of your evening activity.

FOXES YOUTH

Were we to return to FEAR CITY today (if we ever left . . .), then the cautionary advice would have to be updated – "Hide your iPad/laptop/smartphone", "Don't text and drive", "Look UP! Look where you're GOING!" So yes, take this good advice next time you walk any city's streets. Look closer, for THEY are ever-present all around you – Skulls Are Everywhere! Much like the Mobile Phone Zombies . . .

Photos © ILYA, 2013

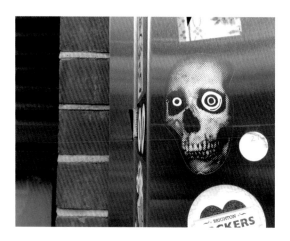

Street art can take many forms, but the two most common are 1. sticker bombing, and 2. painted murals (usually large scale) – both manifestations, micro to macro, witnessed here in Kensington Street, Brighton, UK.

The appearance of one usually leads to more: the impromptu gallery space, once declared, soon confirmed.

Top
RX SKULLS shares with the world, Kensington Street, Brighton, UK.

Above
Ali Bongo Rests in Pieces / Primeval Soup

Opposite
One for MOM

Photos © ILYA, 2013

Opposite
Two-part skull image, Noah
Scalin, spraypainted stencil art
www.skulladay.blogspot.com

Top
Graffiti – from the Limelight
Club, London, caught just
before it disappears forever

beneath refurbishment.
Photo by Rian Hughes

Bottom
Matthew Bromley Panel Piece,
Café 1001 grill stand, just off
Brick Lane, London.
Photo by ILYA
www.madebybromley.com

DAVE THE CHIMP

Prolific Dave the Chimp paints graffiti without his name, and makes fanzines to switch on your brain (titles include Dang, Check My Chops, Headbone, and Recycle Ya Bastards). A founder member of the Finders Keepers Crew (along with D*Face, PMH, and Mysterious Al) he continues to bomb the streets under a plethora of secret identities. "Painting and skating keep the noose from around my neck," he says.

Here's some skulls.

www.davethechimp.co.uk

Top left
Fortress Chimp

Top right
ViceLord

Opposite, clockwise from top left
Anatomy of Man

Mural hack

Chimp Cyclops Sweettoof

Street skulls, London

"This is my take on Damien Hirst's bejewelled child skull.* I don't have millions to spend on diamonds. All I have of worth are my characters."

Dave the Chimp.

* For the Love of God, a platinum skull set with diamonds, 2007

Left
FtLoG REMIX.

Opposite
For the Love of Gawd

Opposite
Gone Done Wrong, painting

Below
Street skulls, Germany

"The Street Skulls from Germany relate to the *Gone Done Wrong* piece. It's a character I was drawing in secret places, and I didn't tell anyone it was me."

Dave the Chimp

KLONE

Born (or perhaps cloned) 1983 in Harkov, Ukraine, former USSR, Klone Yourself nowadays resides in Tel Aviv, Israel. His work deals with memories, his own and those of his surroundings, past or present – the layers of the city, walls crumbling apart, graffiti covering and being covered, people getting old and the new generations appearing every moment. "I learn a new language that invents itself along the way," he says.

www.kloneyourself.com
www.instagram.com/kloneyourself

KLONE
YOURSELF
SCU SERIES

Opposite
Scu11

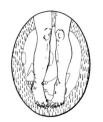

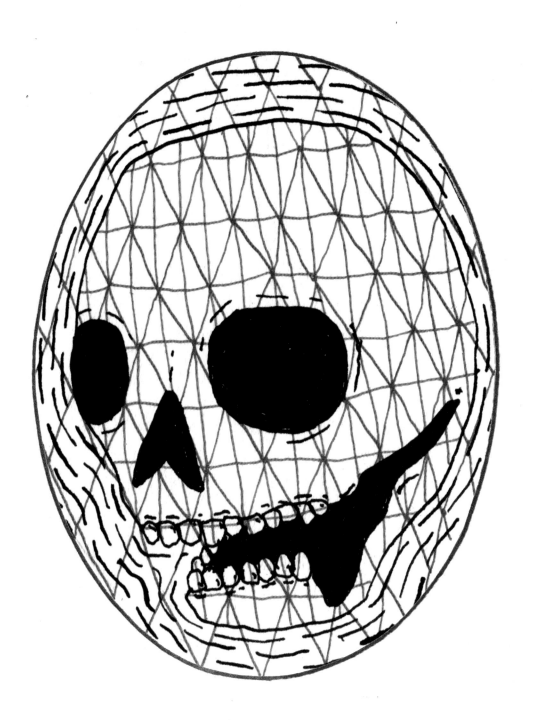

RX SKULLS

Baron Von Sticker

Self-confessed total adhesive junkie, RX SKULLS (or ARREX) is all about the handmade, hand-printed and hand-cut. "Almost all of my artwork features different renditions of the same exact skull which I photographed in a London museum over five years ago. I share my skull image with the world as a little morbid reminder to everyone to live each day. *Memento Mori*. My aim is also to prove that despite the skull's overuse in popular culture . . . it can still be a visceral image, especially in its beautiful simplicity." Amen to that.

www.arrex.bigcartel.com

Top left, opposite and following spreads
Photos by RX.

Top right
Photos by Nick Morgan.

"99 per cent of my stickers are silk-screened, printed by hand by me, and cut with a trusty pair of scissors. I love photos of my stickers that you can tell have been on the street for a while – weathered by time, or by individuals."

Arrex, RX SKULLS

JASON MIDAS MITCHELL

Jason Mitchell is punk rock and hardcore. He works in New York City under the moniker Midas Images, and as part of the Urban Folk Art collective.

Jason's iconic skull scroll design, *Lone skroull on a black field*, was also printed and disseminated as a 3 in. circular sticker (above).

These day and night sticker shots (following pages) are anchored by two views of the famous Cyclone ride, in Coney Island's theme park, New York City. On the top of the pole are Obey stickers by Shepard Fairey (one of Jason's Rhode Island School of Design roommates). Below his work are stickers for one of Jason's many punk bands, AS$TROLAND.

See also: Art Skulls

Above
Stickerone

Opposite
Stickers Day composite

Below

Jason's drawing *Till Anti* has see-through tooth roots. Eyes, teeth, skulls (obviously), music and letterforms are all constant sources of inspiration. As with almost every street artist alive, the seminal work and freeflow line of the late Vaughn Bode can be found somewhere in his DNA.

Opposite

Other stuck sticker images in this night-time selection include another of Jason's bands, MISCEGENATOR. He says, "I have friends around the world putting stickers up – as you can see from online posts that go from San Francisco to Ireland."

Above

Urban Folk Art Halloween
show poster, by Jason MIDAS
Mitchell. Jason's currently
working on making more
skulls for future shows.
Good man!

Right

Rollerjaw comes from Jason
Mitchell's Sketchbook project.
For a fee, the sketchbooks
are mailed out, to be filled
and returned. They are then
digitized and displayed online,
as well as touring the world to
be held and enjoyed.

jsnmidas.tumblr.com

JUL 15 2013

SWEET TOOF

Whether solo or in collaboration, Sweet Toof's studio artworks evolve out of his urban graffiti – tags, throw-ups, and more elaborate street pieces. Fusing ancient methods with modern materials, he glosses urban detritus with a bygone decadence. A master of the formula: traditional + contemporary = unconventional x iconoclastic!

www.sweettoof.com

Top left
Portrait of the Artist

Top right
Metro

Bottom
Railyard Bulls

Opposite
The Client

Two more stencil skulls from ever-active Noah Scalin.
www.skulladay.blogspot.co.uk

Opposite
Stencil no.1: Spray paint on corrugated metal. Stencil based on a photo taken in the Catacombs beneath Paris (very much worth a visit).

On this page
Stylized stencil skull: Spray-painted stencil on wall. Online comments range from "That's an eggsellent skull!" to "Very Banksy!"

TATTOO SKULLS

Skulls of every sort – piratical, rotting, writhing with serpents – have been a perennial favourite among folks sporting tattoos ever since body art was first invented. Nowadays even kids want to get in on the act – see opposite – although with strictly temporary versions.

The tattooists who design and make these enduring images are talented artists in their own right, often exhibiting their own drawings and paintings – beyond flesh – as an advertisement of their skills.

Top, left to right
THE TRIBE – temporary tattoo, street find. "Live on the Road, Die on the Road"

WWE (World Wrestling Entertainment) star Brock Lesnar sweatily sports an evil skull back tattoo

Original design by Tommi Musturi

Right and opposite
Ed Hardy TATTOOS – yes, your kid too can wear a broken heart on their (washable) sleeve that bears the legend LOVE KILLS SLOWLY

Ed Hardy™ TATTOOS

Ed Hardy is a registered trademark of Hardy Way LLC. Copyright to all images owned by Hardy Way LLC.

4+

30+ TATTOOS · TATOUAGES · TATUAJES

30 TATTOOS · TATOUAGES · TATUAJES

⚠ **WARNING:**
CHOKING HAZARD-Small parts.
Not for children under 3 years.

⚠ **AVERTISSEMENT:**
DANGER D'ÉTOUFFEMENT- Petites piéces.
Pas pour les enfants de moins de 3 ans.

⚠ **ADVERTENCIA:**
PELIGRO DE ATRAGANTAMIENTO - Piezas
pequeñas. No es para niños menores de 3 años.

NIA

Chasing down a contact on a cool tattoo-style image of a demon, found stickered in East London, led us to Nia. Simply identified "Girl from Rotterdam" (in the Netherlands), she nonetheless leapt at the chance to do a brand-new skull commission especially for this book. Currently making paintings and prints, Nia's not tattooing yet – she's still looking for a tattoo apprenticeship at the moment – but she takes requests, and sells her artwork online.

www.vivalania.com
www.facebook.com/vivalania
www.instagram.com/vivalania

Artwork © 2013 Nia –
Rotterdam, NL.
Watercolour, drawing ink and
Edding permanent markers

JAN WILLEM

Nia (previous spread) in turn recommended Jan Willem of *25 To Life Tattoos*, also found in Rotterdam, and once we saw his artworks we were left in no doubt: here he is.

www.jwtattooer.com

www.instagram.com/jwx

Left
Fatty Skull

Below, left to right
Skull, Skull rose, Lady skullhat

**Opposite clockwise
from top left**
Skull fire, Skull coffin, Skull frame, Axe boy, Skull fire

All images
© Jan Willem, Tattooer. Photographs by tattoo artists always look a little raw, skin angry and flushed, because they are taken when the tattoo's just been done. Ouch!

304

Above
Japanese Reaper study

Opposite
Japanese Reaper

KORE FLATMO

Any approaches to other tattoo artists effectively ended the day we found Kore Flatmo. When it comes to Skull tattoos, he's The Boss: the ultimate, the very last word.

Tucked away in an interesting older neighborhood, off the beaten path, in Cincinnati, Ohio, USA, PluraBella was established in 1999 as a private studio for tattoo veteran, Kore – 30 years in the business – in which to create his original tattoos, expressly tailored to the individual.

Aside from his speciality, full-coverage tattoos, LA native Kore also produces deceptively delicate watercolour paintings, charcoal drawings, custom etchings and, most recently, wood engravings and pyrography (literally "writing with fire"). His wife and business partner, tattoo artist Brenda, also displays a mean line in Rock portraiture (Johnny Cash, Nick Cave . . .).

www.plurabella.com
www.brendaflatmo.com

Opposite
Torso tattoo, Jason, circa 2006

Top
Multi tattoo, Chris, circa 2010

Bottom
Couple tattoo, Eric, circa 2012

Top
Salva Res Est ("All's Well"), 2011

Bottom left
The Skeleton and the Veil, 2010

Bottom right
Wanna Split a Popsicle? 2009

Opposite
Last Gasp, 2000

All paintings by Kore Flatmo

Gentle Lady, 2011

Opposite
Puccini, 2011

Right
Coffin, 2012

Opposite
Dragon Skull, 2012

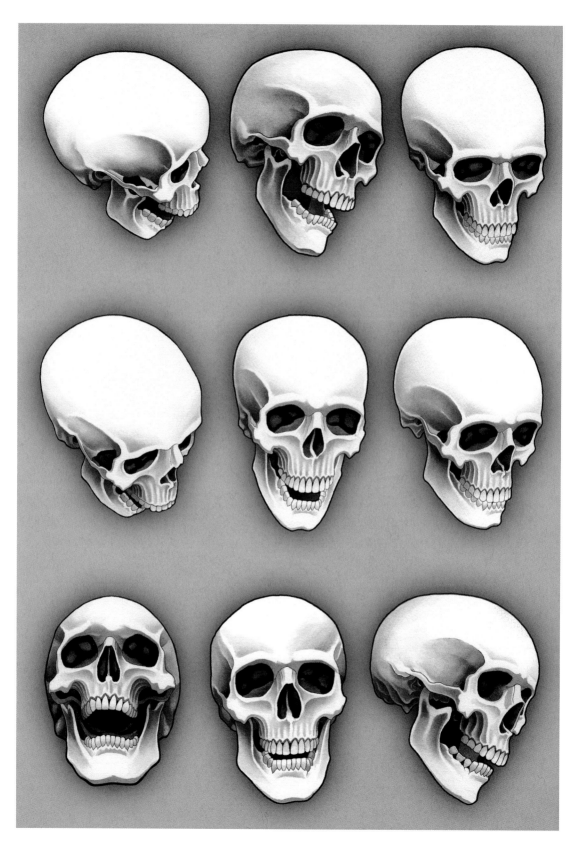

Opposite
Kore Flatmo published a book through PluraBella, *18 Angles of the Human Skull*, which has become something of a bible in its own right among the cognoscenti – for reasons that should be immediately obvious. You are lucky enough to see some of it right here …

18 Angles of the Human Skull, page 4: Kore Flatmo is such a serious student of human anatomy that he has become its master, both inside and out!

Top
Skeleton, 2011

Right
Skull book cover, 2005

Right
Skull tattoo, Tim, circa 2011

Opposite
Side tattoo, Sterling,
circa 2009

All tattoos by Kore Flatmo

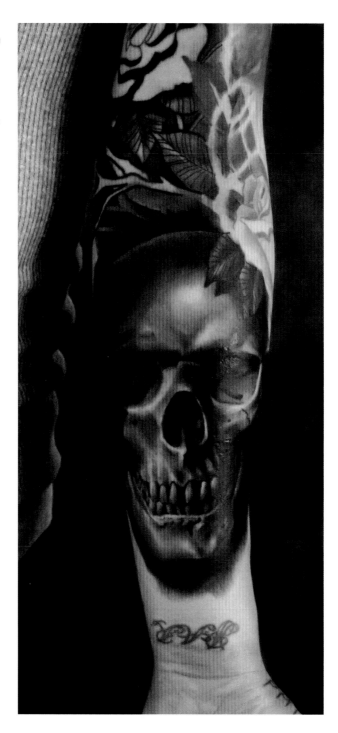

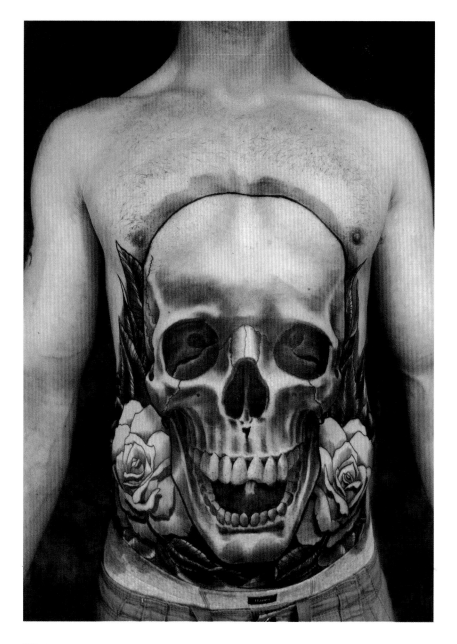

Above
Chest tattoo, Kevin, circa 2013

Opposite
Skeleton Back, Kurt, circa 2010

ROCK'N'ROLL SKULLS

"We all will feed the worms and trees so don't be shy
Swallow and chew, eat you alive
All of us food, that hasn't died"

"Mosquito Song", Queens of the Stone Age

Skull imagery and Rock 'n' Roll/Metal music go together like booze and smokes, cheese and onion, death and taxes. The Sons of Anarchy use it to express their rebellion and devil-may-care attitude. Iron Maiden's rotted mascot, Eddie, is recognized the world over. Danzig, Guns'n'Roses . . . we could go on. Why fade away, when you can flame out. Live Free or Die!

Top, left to right
Hessen Metal logo by Dave
the Chimp. "I made this in
2000 for Mob skateboards.
They still use it. The designers
at Zoo York said I'd 'killed it' for
skull logos for the next
ten years!"

Night club flyer for Zombie
Rockin'

Spine graphic from
Supersonic, Visuals for Music
© Die Gestalten Verlag GmbH,
Berlin, 2007
www.die-gestalten.de

Bottom
Sons of Anarchy season 5 skull
logo © FX network

Opposite
Night club flyer for The Crobar,
Soho, London

THE CROBAR
SOHO, LONDON

LONDON'S BEST LATE-NIGHT BEER N' WHISKEY ROCK N' ROLL BAR IN THE HEART OF SOHO

OPEN UNTIL 3AM MON-SAT. ENTRY £2 AFTER 11

BOURBON AND MIXER £2.50 ALL NIGHT MON-THURS

Magnificent Glorification Of Lucife

message
from books
and dreams

Top row, left to right
Atrophy, *Violent by Nature* LP,
RoadRacer Records.
Cover illustration by
Paul Stottler. Thrash Metal

Angkor Wrack, *Cult Pump*
(Denmark, 2011) – 7" vinyl
sleeve, Limited Edition.
Post-Punk

Sons of Anarchy logo
© FX network
"You've gotta earn your
patch!"

Middle row, left to right
Inquisition, *the Magnificent
Glorification of Lucifer* LP,
No Colors Records, cover
illustration by Antichrist
Kramer. Black Metal.
"The singer sounds like a
frog, and the music is trancey,
mesmerizing, menacing.
I love it!" – Smo

Oltretomba – 7 inch single –
Zven Balslev/Soren Mosdal.
Named after the Italian horror
comic (300 issues, 1971 to
1986) – meaning: afterlife,
hereafter, next world. Check
online for many great pulp
cover paintings.

"I have a weak spot for clumsy
heavy metal art, which I think
sometimes approaches folk
art, in a way" – Smo.
Skullfinder General: Smo
(Soren Mosdal). Scans: Frøydis
Sollid Simonsen

Night club flyer for Voodoo
Rock, London

Bottom row, left to right
Iron Maiden, debut album by
the eponymous British heavy
metal band, 1980. The origin
of Eddie! Artwork by
Derek Riggs

Message, From Books and
Dreams, Psychedelic/Space
Rock/Progressive Rock from
1973

EMEK

"The Thinking Man's Poster Artist"

Art Major Emek is the undisputed King of Skulls. For the last
20 years, his concert poster designs have rocked the world
– combining trademark psychedelic imagery reminiscent of
the 1960s with cutting-edge post-industrial hardcore, organic
mass with robotic sharp edges. Clients include the Beastie Boys,
Flaming Lips, painted album covers for Neil Young, Pearl Jam,
plus many punk and alternative bands. The same committed
intensity carries over from Emek's music posters to his protest
art and illustration – socially conscious, yet fantastical and
often humourous.

www.emek.net

Top left
The Art of Punk, original punk
art from the 70s, 80s and 90s

Top right
High on Fire

Opposite
The Flaming Lips, Bookish

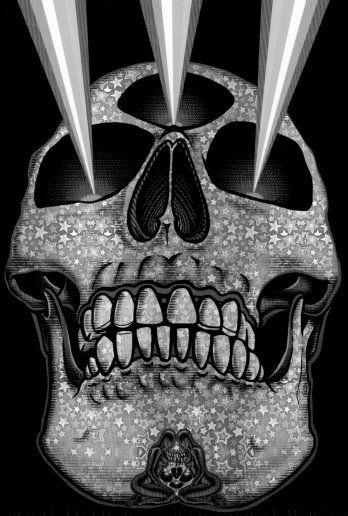

THE FLAMING LIPS

SATURDAY JULY 27 2013 MCMENAMINS EDGEFIELD TROUTDALE OREGON

Left
Graphics for Queens of the
Stone Age

Opposite
Dope concert poster

Emek first draws by hand, then silkscreens his plastic-fantastic
images onto paper, usually in limited editions of around 300.
Never one to rest on his laurels, he also experiments with actual
metal, glass, you name it – even carving in stone.

Billboard magazine's Top 25 rock posters of all time include three by Emek, his work permanently displayed in branches of the Hard Rock Café, as well as shown in galleries across the United States, in Berlin, London and Tokyo.

Left
The Fantomas poster

Right
Deadmaus poster

Opposite
Bauhaus concert poster,
Manchester, UK.

Following spread
Stamped metal and
aluminium graphics for the
Foo Fighters

332

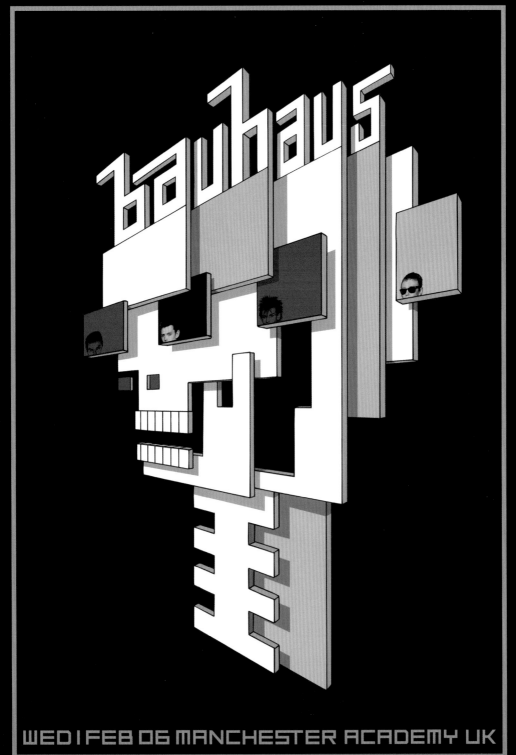

WED I FEB 06 MANCHESTER ACADEMY UK

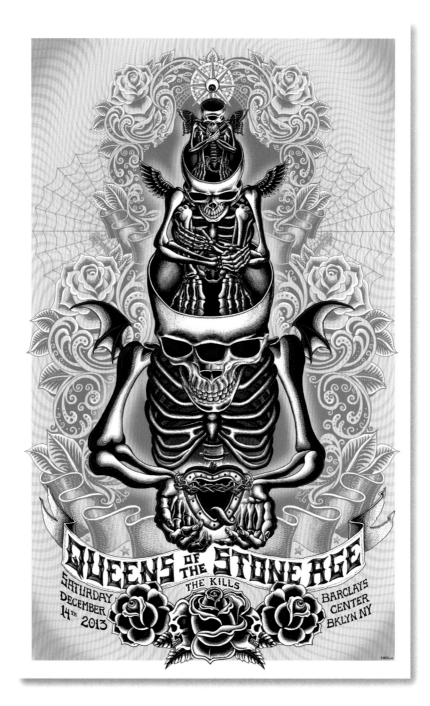

Above and opposite

Graphics for Queens of the
Stone Age

QUEENS OF THE STONE AGE
TURBONEGRO

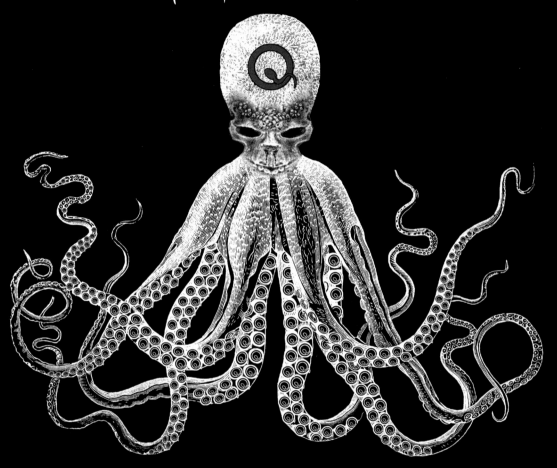

MARQUEE THEATRE
03·17·03
JACKSONVILLE FLORIDA

P.N.E./QOTSA-17

Opposite and above
Branding graphics for ZZ Top

Above
Graphics for Queens of the
Stone Age

Opposite
zzz soulstealer book

RYAN CLARK

Invisible Creature

Founded in 2006 by brothers Don and Ryan Clark, Invisible Creature is a multi-disciplinary design and illustration studio based in Seattle, Washington, USA.

"From very early in our childhood, we knew exactly what we wanted to do with our lives," says Ryan. From doodling in the margins of school textbooks (you too?), via punk rock (er, yup!), that same passion now manifests itself in sleeve design, illustration and urban vinyl (toys!). Rockers in real life, the dynamic sibling duo have received 4 Grammy nominations for their music packaging. Besides the obvious skull fetish, Ryan also grooves on religious imagery, fashion, graffiti, 90s' music, skateboard culture, comics and tattoos. Our kinda guy . . .

www.invisiblecreature.com

Top left
MyChildren MyBride, page from album artwork.
Design by Ryan Clark for Invisible Creature, Inc.
Photography by Jerad Knudson
Solid State Records

Above and opposite
Fear Factory – silkscreened tour posters.
Design by Ryan Clark for Invisible Creature, Inc.

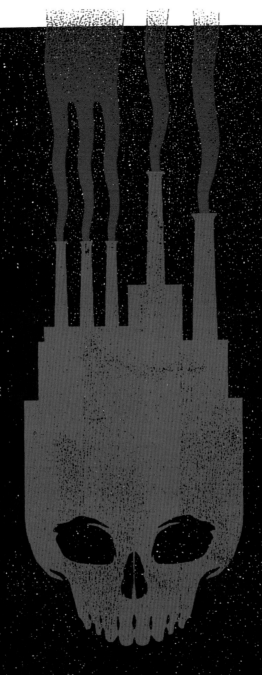

FEAR·FACTORY

SOILWORK · STRAPPING YOUNG LAD · DARKANE

· Sunday December 1, 2002 / 7:30pm / El Corazon / 109 Eastlake Ave E / 206-262-0482 / All Ages / $18 ·

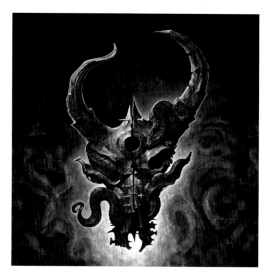

Top row, left to right

Alice In Chains – *The Devil Put Dinosaurs Here* album cover. (two images – red jewel case and reveal).
Design by Ryan Clark for Invisible Creature, Inc.
Capitol Records

To Speak Of Wolves – *Find Your Worth, Come Home* album cover.
Design by Ryan Clark for Invisible Creature, Inc.
Solid State Records

Middle row, left to right

Demon Hunter – *Summer Of Darkness* album cover.
Design by Michael Christian McCaddon.
Solid State Records

Demon Hunter – *The Triptych* album cover.
Illustration by Dan Seagrave.
Solid State Records

The Agony Scene – *Get Damned* album cover.
Illustration by Ryan Clark for Invisible Creature, Inc.
Century Media Records

Bottom row, left to right

Demon Hunter – *True Defiance* album cover.
Illustration by Justin Kamerer/ Angryblue.
Solid State Records

My Heart To Fear – *Lost Between Brilliance And Insanity* album cover.
Design by Ryan Clark for Invisible Creature, Inc.
Solid State Records

Bleeding Through – *Bleeding Through* album cover.
Illustration by Ryan Clark for Invisible Creature, Inc.
Rise Records

Left
The Ascendicate – *To Die As Kings* album cover.
Design by Ryan Clark for Invisible Creature, Inc.
Solid State Records

Top right
August Burns Red – *Thrill Seeker* album cover.
Design by Ryan Clark for Invisible Creature, Inc.
Solid State Records

Bottom
DevilDriver – *Winter Kills* album cover.
Design by Ryan Clark for Invisible Creature, Inc.
Photography by Dean Karr.
Napalm Records

Opposite
The Agony Scene – silkscreened tour poster.
Design by Ryan Clark for Invisible Creature, Inc.

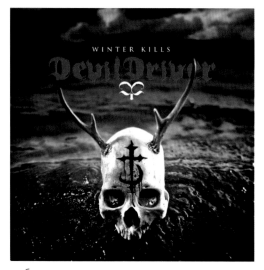

THE AGONY SCENE

NODES OF RANVIER / SCARLET / BECOMING THE ARCHETYPE

on tour now

DYLAN GARRETT SMITH

Artist, occultist, collector, Dylan digs skulls. He emerged from the punk and hardcore scene of north-east Pennsylvania, USA – experimenting from an early age with printmaking to create shirts and patches for friends' bands, including his own, using very basic materials like cardboard stencils and spray paint. Nowadays, with a Bachelor's Degree in Fine Arts from the Pratt Institute in Brooklyn, Smith draws, using ashes, chalk lead and ink to make dark magic. In particular, he likes to comment on the growing distance between humans and the natural world. (Kudos to Daniel Emerson, New Art.)

www.instagram.com/dylanxvx

Top
Belial

Opposite
Dying

Top and bottom left
Memento Mori

Check out Dylan's website for
more of his shirt designs.

Below right
Dhegem

Opposite
Early Graves

EARLY GRAVES

"I have a collection of human and animal skulls, so every photographic image was taken and edited by me using skulls from my collection."

Dylan Garrett Smith

Equinox Ritual I and *II*

JON LANGFORD

Long-time founding member of legendary British rock group, the Mekons, Langford, native to South Wales, now lives in Chicago, USA.

"All the experiences I'd had with the evil music biz monster sort of bubbled up into my work," says the artist. "The art and the music definitely come from the same part of the brain and form the bulk of my creative output." His oeuvre? "Bourbon-drenched bar room frieze frames from the classic age of honky-tonk music, when men were drunk and the women were feisty", according to Dogfish Head brewery's Sam Calagione, who first admired Jon's paintings on the walls of the Windy City's rock and beer emporium, Delilah's. Langford continues to play with the Mekons, Chicago band the Waco Brothers, and his own Skull Orchard.

www.jonlangford.de

www.yarddog.com

Top, left to right
Going Down In History

Jack A Diamonds

We Never Knew We Had So Many Friends, an etching based on a Mekons song called 'Coal Hole' – "*Hank is dead, the strike is over…*" inking the fate of Hank Williams with his own Welsh heritage.

Opposite
Lofty Deeds, 'all the fame of Lofty Deeds must perish like a dream'

Above
Lofty Skull

Opposite
All Roads

Following spread
Without a Doubt,
"one of my US Foreign policy
paintings", quite possibly
co-starring The Duke.

Back to those skeletons . . . why all the death?
"The Waco Brothers had a song about the death of country
music, and I liked the idea of Mexican Day of the Dead art
and old Dutch vanitas etchings and paintings – rich blokes
sitting at their tables with skulls, egg-timers, candles
burning down. Ominous stuff . . . you can't take it with you!"

Jon Langford interviewed at www.dogfish.com

Above
Copy of Lofty Scratched

Opposite
Hank Immortal

Top
Moon Sun Cowgirl

Bottom
Skull Girl Gold

Opposite
Skull Girl on Fence 300

If you like these, be sure to check out Jon Langford's monograph, Nashville Radio, from Verse Chorus Press, USA.

362

MUTOID WASTE

Original stickers and flyer for an all-night warehouse party (what would later become known as illegal raves), early 1980s – this one a literal demolition derby taking place in a derelict postal service sorting office, with the audience on a vast concrete island in the middle. A great time had by all and – get this, Health and Safety Executive – no-one hurt!

The Mutoids are still active today: welding sculptures from waste materials and custom-building Mad Max vehicles, they took part in the closing ceremony for the 2012 Summer Paralympics.

Opposite
Elvis, was a hero to some … Rollermania – back page ad from 1980s' Bristol, UK skatepunk zine Skate Muties from the 5th Dimension by Bear (lead singer of the UK punk group Lunatic Fringe) and his brother Beano – nowadays screenprinting and shooting videos for the likes of Radiohead and The Scissor Sisters. Skate Muties … they came from outer space to destroy heroes!

Following spread
South London's supremo Lord Hurk shares a before and afterlife shot for a hard riding Son of Anarchy.

www.lordhurk.com

-ATTENTION!-
WE HAVE FOUND HIM!

YES, THE REAL ELVIS IS BACK AND WORKING AT
ROLLERMANIA
EXCEEDS THE NEED

HAPPENING AT: 62 PARK ROW BRISTOL BS15LE TEL.(0272)279981 -TUE-SAT

NATURAL SELECTION

Noah Scalin

The *Natural Selection* portrait series explores the lives of great scientists whose work has had an incredible impact on the world. Each diptych is made up of the portrait of a deceased scientist, and a representation of their skull. The skull is made by literally rearranging the elements used in the portrait, thus destroying that original creation, in the spirit of the traditional sand mandalas of Tibetan Buddhism.

The scientists represented are all great thinkers whose ideas had an impact on our lives today, but also have serious repercussions in their own lives (and deaths).

www.noahscalin.com/work/natural-selection

Darwin, feathers

Charles Darwin (1809–1882) developed the theory of evolution by natural selection, which he based in part on observations of birds in the Galápagos. The theory was nearly universally accepted by scientists by the time he died, but has been consistently refuted by religious fundamentalists ever since.

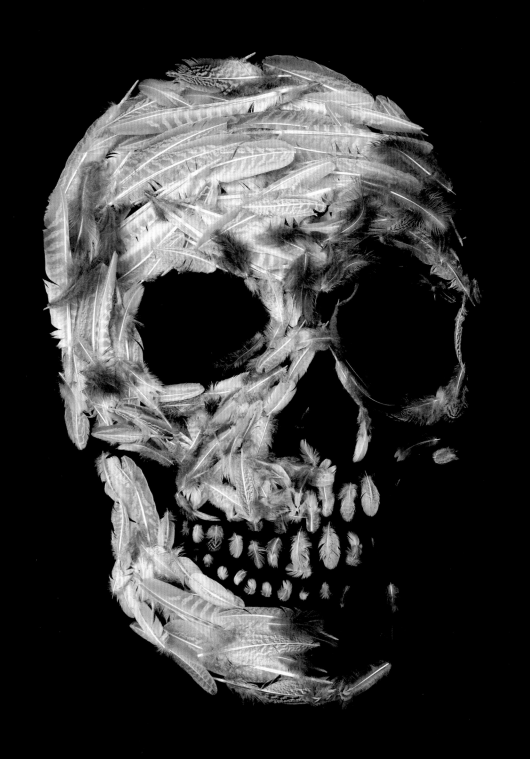

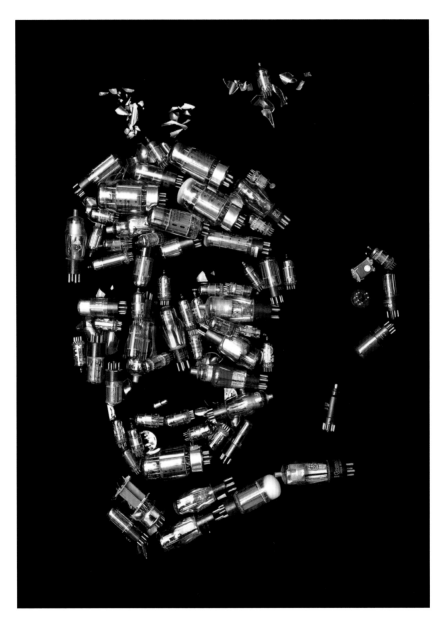

Tesla, vacuum tubes

Nikola Tesla (1856–1943), prolific inventor, developed alternating current (AC), was hugely famous in his lifetime, but died impoverished, in debt and mostly forgotten.

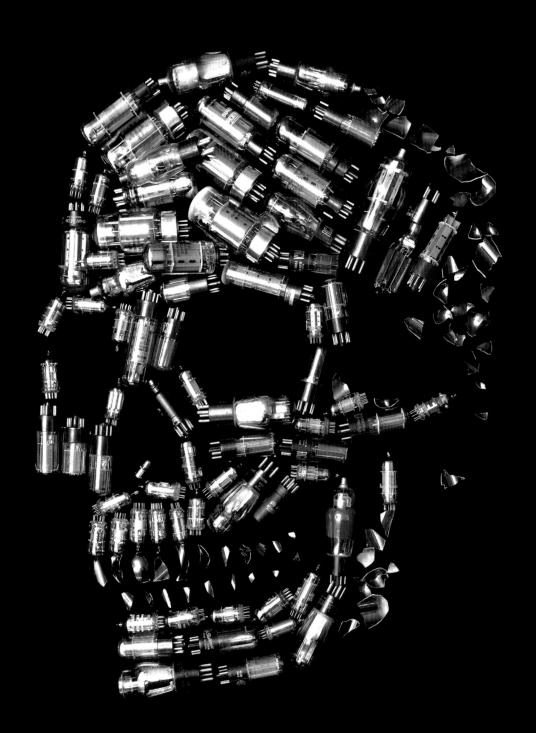

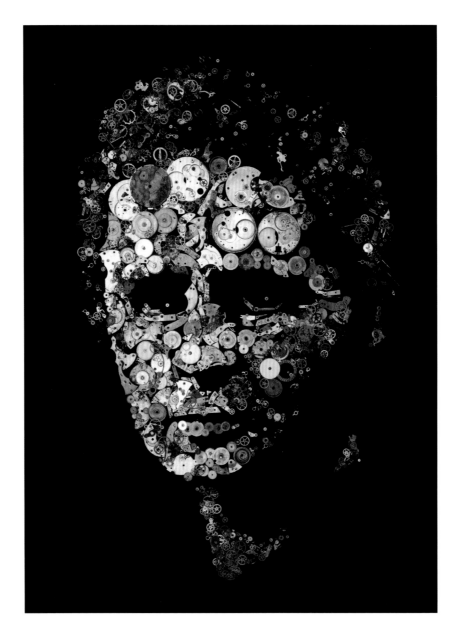

Curie, watch parts, including radium painted hands

Marie Curie (1867–1934) developed the theory of radioactivity and fundamentally changed modern physics and chemistry, becoming the first woman to win a Nobel Prize. Extended exposure to radiation from her work ultimately caused her death, and to this day her papers are so radioactive they have to be kept in lead-lined boxes, and only handled while wearing protective gear.

Einstein, dice

Albert Einstein (1879–1955) developed the general theory of relativity and the most famous of all equations, $E=mc^2$, but died refusing to accept the concepts behind quantum mechanics, saying many times, "God doesn't play dice with the world".

Turing, computer keys

Alan Turing (1912–1954) developed the concepts that led to modern computing, and was fundamental in cracking Nazi codes in the Second World War, but was persecuted by the UK government for his homosexuality and ultimately committed suicide.

Franklin, chandelier crystals

Rosalind Franklin (1920–1958) primarily known for her work as an X-ray crystallographer, made a key discovery that led to the modern understanding of the structure of DNA. However her work was used without permission or credit and she died without Nobel Prize recognition.

Top left
Skull chandelier by Zeel
www.zeel.co.uk

Bottom right
Woody – carved wood
skeleton by Zeel

Right
White and Red Roman skulls
Photo: Rian Hughes

SKULLPTURE*

Skulls, human or otherwise, are a part of the skeleton – the scaffold, as it were, that the body hangs from. This makes it a natural subject for sculpture; whether as subject or even as raw material.

From monumental skulls, found in graveyards, to architectural features and forms around and above us on the city streets, weirdling interior decorations and perverse artefacts, that distinctive shape – sockets gaping, cheekbones jutting – is ever-present. Yet, in this section, we arrive at some of the most unexpected and unusual skulls of all – baked in bread, moulded in chocolate and cake icing, made of light, or teddy bear terrifying – the most effective perhaps for being three-dimensional and, thus, so much more closely resembling the real thing.

*Whoa, bad pun! Well, perhaps, but Momma taught me never to look a gift horse in the mouth and count how many teeth it had.

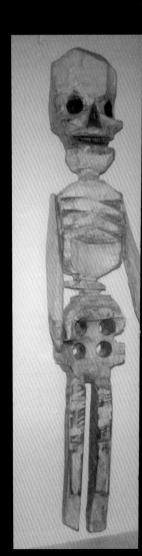

Top right
Funeral Directors, Zeel,
Crafted wood and plastic toy.
Note the acid bath in back!

Centre
Alter Suedfriedhof, Munich,
Germany. Photo by Veronika
Streitwieser

Right
Bone chandelier, Sedlec
Ossuary, Kutná Hora,
Czech Republic
www.ossuary.eu
Photo by Lette Anina
(Lettanina)

JESSICA JOSLIN

The creatures that populate Jessica Joslin's world are intricate fusions of bone, brass, antique hardware and other scavenged treasures. They reflect animals both real and imagined, the living and the dead – animates and reanimates infused with a passion for natural history in combination with arcane technology. In this, they are eerily reminiscent of enthusiasms and the Cabinets of Curiosity of the Victorian Era. Think also of *The Time Machine*, from the 1960 George Pal film based on the H. G. Wells novel of the same name – crossed with birds, or beasts!

Jessica Joslin began building her bestiary of mechanical animals in 1992, and her creature collection now numbers over 200 sculptures. With an extensive background in the professional trades, the Chicago-based artist honed her fabrication skills building toy prototypes, architectural models, trade show displays, photo props and film sets.

Top
858, Antique hardware, silver, brass, bone, embroidered velvet, glove leather, glass eyes.
14 x 10 x 10 in.

Opposite
Cisco, Antique hardware and findings, brass, silver, bone, painted steel, glove leather, glass eyes.
20 x 10 x 18 in.
Photos by Jessica Joslin

Antique chandeliers are dissected and reconfigured into anatomical forms. Candy dishes are fashioned into rib-cages. Silver forks are cut, bent, and bolted back together to form articulated monkey toes. The spout of a teapot becomes a fish's tail. A skull from a cat might be altered to resemble a monkey, or a chicken might be given a new beak to resemble an exotic bird.

Collecting, assembing and exhibiting works in the tradition of figures as diverse as Sir Hans Sloane and the great showman, P. T. Barnum, Joslin has been christened on Facebook a "Millennial Geppetto" (the woodcarver who made Pinocchio).

Some of the bones are real, some are not. "For all protected and endangered species, I create replicas," says Joslin. "For the sculptures that incorporate real animal bones, I work with licensed osteological suppliers, such as skullsunlimited.com. Other elements, I find everywhere! I am always searching for interesting objects at flea markets, on eBay, or at dozens of specialty hardware suppliers. I use everything from antique lamps and textiles, to unusual period cutlery, to parasol parts and brass bullet casings. There isn't any single source."

Top left
Violet & Cordula, antique hardware and findings, brass, silver, bone, cast pewter, painted wood, glove leather, glass eyes
9 x 6 x 4 in.

Right
Tapio, antique hardware and findings, brass, bone, vintage chain, glove leather, glass eyes.
5.5 x 3 x 1.25 in.

Below
Jacques, antique silver, bone, turtle shell, glove leather, glass eyes
4 x 3 x 1.5 in.

Above
Troy, antique hardware and findings, brass, silver, bone, vestment trim,velvet, musical instrument parts, painted steel. glove leather, glass eyes

Above

Cooper, antique hardware,
chandelier parts, silver, brass,
cast pewter, cast plastic, glove
leather, glass eyes
14 x 23 x 20 in.

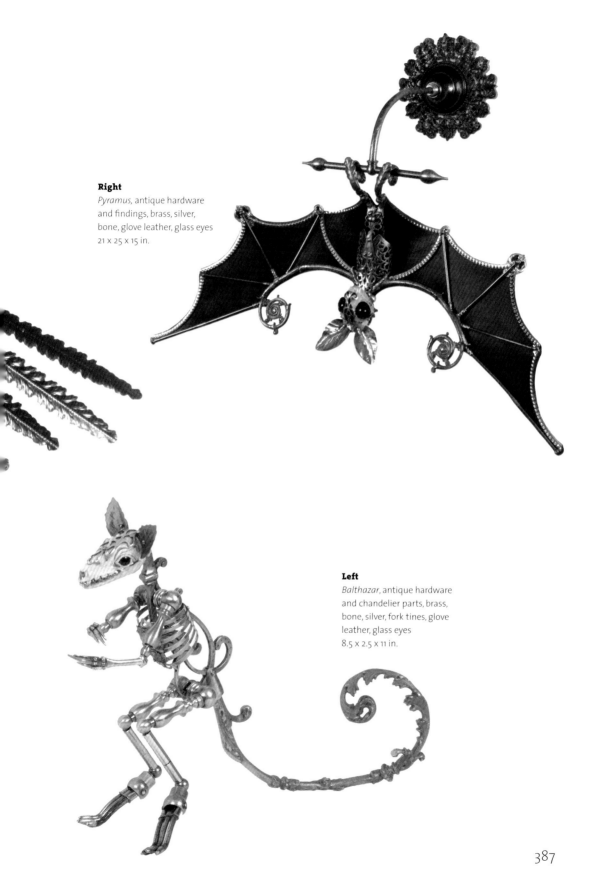

Right
Pyramus, antique hardware
and findings, brass, silver,
bone, glove leather, glass eyes
21 x 25 x 15 in.

Left
Balthazar, antique hardware
and chandelier parts, brass,
bone, silver, fork tines, glove
leather, glass eyes
8.5 x 2.5 x 11 in.

Sculptures range in size from about one inch tall to nearly six feet high. Carefully observed, intricately constructed, these are jewels of the animal and avian kingdoms – effectively re-imagined, crafted, mutated and transmogrified into myriad different species and hybrid forms.

Utilising antique metals – brass, steel, silver and copper – nothing is welded or soldered. Instead, mechanical fastenings – miniature machine bolts, universal joints or couplings are used. Precision engineering conveys a sense that these beasts are anatomically plausible, while limpid glass eyes simulate the spark of life.

Jessica Joslin's monograph, *Strange Nature* was published in 2008. Her work features in numerous books, magazines and exhibitions worldwide.

www.jessicajoslin.com

Top left
Claudius, antique silver, brass hardware, velvet trim, cast plastic, vintage glove leather, glass eyes
5.5 x 6.5 x 6 in.

Opposite
Rudolph, antique hardware and findings, brass horn, bone, antlers, beads, silver, vestment trim, glove leather, glass eyes
17 x 10 x 13 in.

389

STEPHANIE METZ

Stephanie Metz received her BFA in Sculpture at the University of Oregon. She lives and works in San Jose, California.

The focus of Metz's artwork is overly domesticated creatures, especially those whose form has outgrown – or rather, overgrown – their natural function.

Teddy Bear Natural History, her series of felted wool teddy skulls, explores the imagined anatomy of these traditional children's toys, "symbols of innocence, comfort, and nostalgia. But the teddy bear is also a metaphor for the way humans manipulate the natural world to our own ends. When I had kids, suddenly I was so in touch with the fact that I am a mammal," says Metz.

Top left
Teddy Skull Graphic Girl, Angle,
digital drawing, 2013

Opposite
Ursulus lenis, felted wool,
4.5 x 6.75 x 5 in. 2007
All photographs
© Stephanie Metz

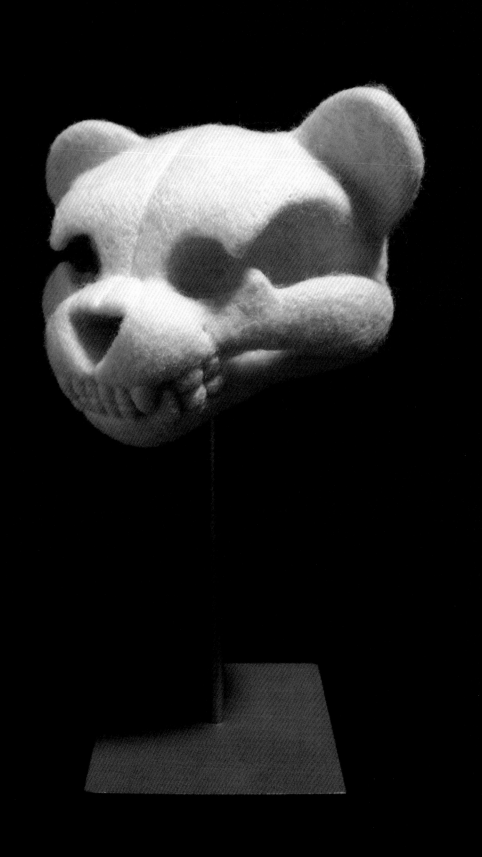

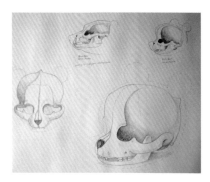
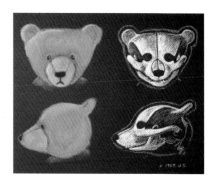

Clockwise, from top left
Teddy Skull Comparative Anatomy Study, graphite on paper, 16 x 22 in. 2006

Teddy Skull Study, c. 1907 U.S., pastel on paper, 12 x 16 in. 2006

Ursulus prolixus, 5.5 x 6.75 x 5.5 in. 2008

Teddy Skull Study, c. 1980 U.S., pastel on paper, 12 x 16 in. 2006

Opposite
Ursulus mellitus, Ursulus queribundus, and *Ursulus gasterpectus,* felted wool, each approximately 6 x 6 x 6 in. 2006

The teddy bear exists as an idea: a docile, cute, friendly invention far removed from the wild animal that inspired it: an irrational and emotionally loaded subject, by design.

To create her Teddy Bear Natural History pieces Stephanie starts with found object toys and reverse engineers physical "evidence" of their biological history in needle-felted wool: a material perfectly suited to representing the fuzzy and soft – yet firm and structural – bones and tissues of stuffed animals. "I borrow heavily from real anatomy," she says.

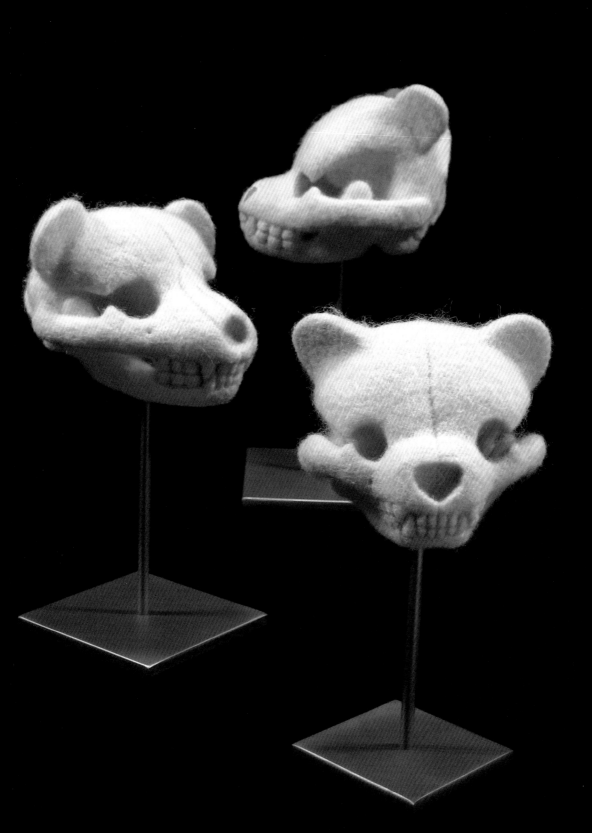

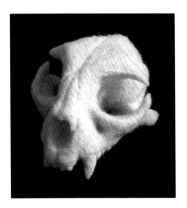 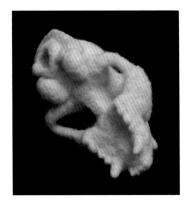 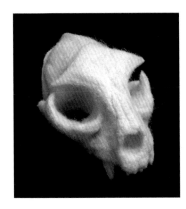

The teddy bear series evolved out of Stephanie's experiments with sheep skulls. "I was interested in looking at the hardest part of the animal and making it out of this soft material. For me, a lot of it is in this dichotomy. Teddy bear anatomy is wholly planned to appeal to the biological response of human adults, to care for their cute, round-featured, helpless babies – a blueprint for bioengineering trends that are taking place today."

Stephanie Metz's numerous group exhibitions include *Creatures: From Bigfoot to the Yeti Crab* at the Sun Valley Center for the Arts in Idaho, *Formex Stockholm 2008* in Stockholm, Sweden, and *Transmission: Experience* at the Institute of Contemporary Arts Gallery, Singapore.

www.stephaniemetz.com
http://www.zazzle.com/stephaniemetz

Above
Cat Skull left angle, *Cat Skull* underside, *Cat Skull* right angle

Opposite
Cat Skull left front angle, *Cat Skull* right, *Cat Skull*, felted wool, 2.5 x 2.5 x 4 in. 2004

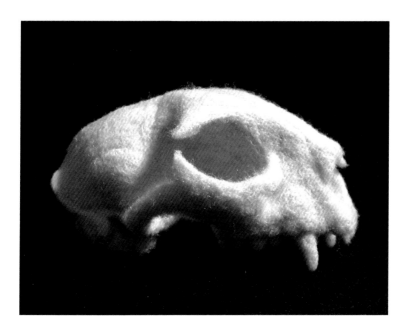

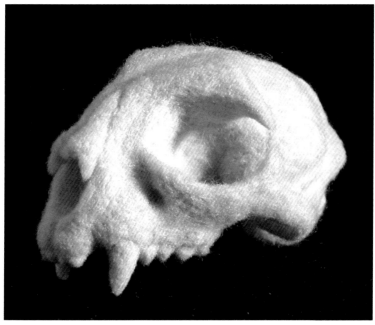

"Sharp canine teeth in a teddy bear skull serve as a reminder that nature can only be tamed to a point."

Stephanie Metz

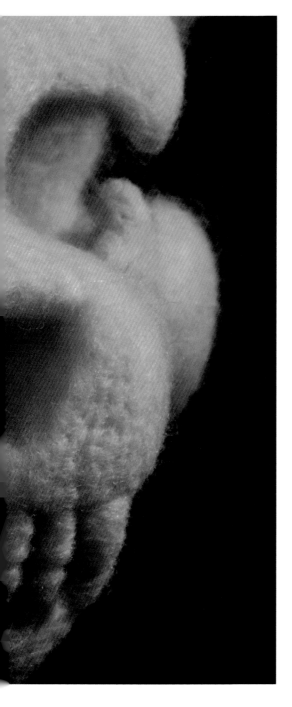

Left

Ursulus lenis, felted wool,
4.5 x 6.75 x 5 in. 2007

Top right

Teddy Skull Graphic, front, digital
drawing, 2013

Introducing Teddy Bear Skull
apparel, now available at the
online store
www.zazzle.com/stephaniemetz

ERIC FRANKLIN

Based in Portland, Oregon, sculptor Eric Franklin is no ordinary glass blower. He constructs stunning anatomical light structures – the human skeletal frame, illuminated from the inside out! A network of flame-worked hollow borosilicate glass tubes – as well as wood and electronics – are filled with a mixture of ionized neon, krypton and mercury gases, causing them to glow, similar to a neon light.

Art installation *Embodiment* took two years to build, from ten different glass units.

www.ericfranklin.com

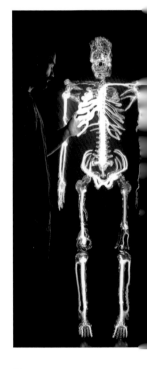

Above
Embodiment

Opposite
Ophelia

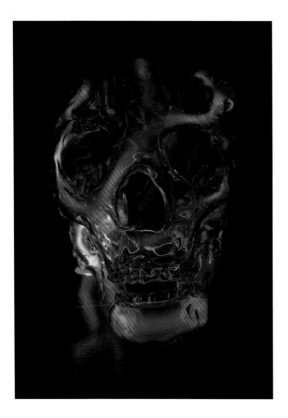

Skull #1

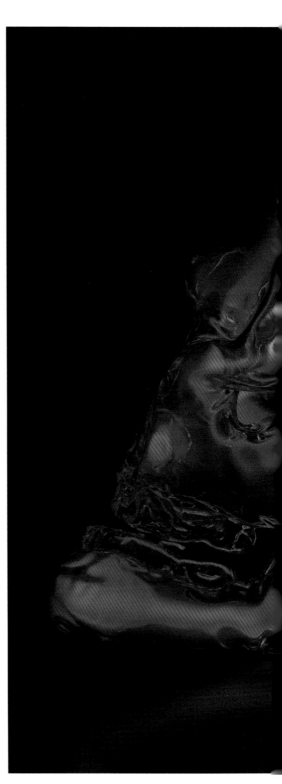

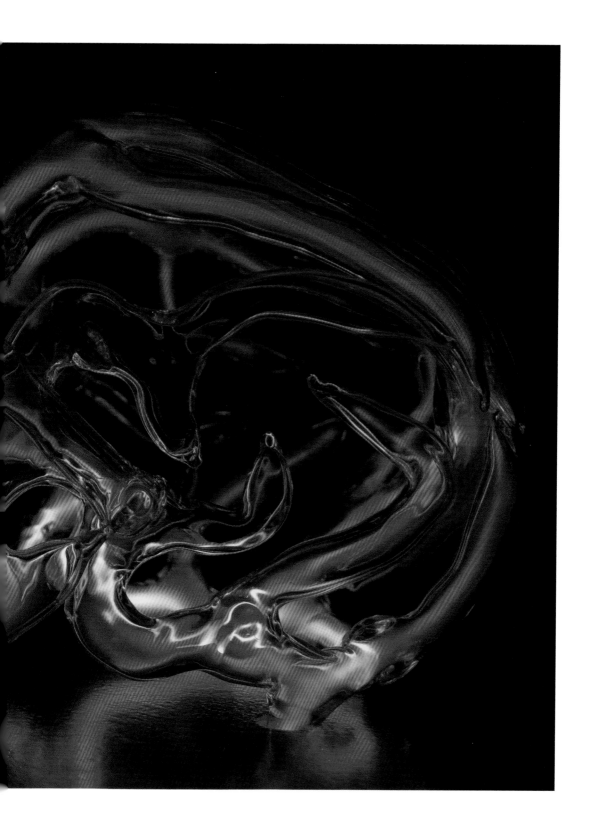

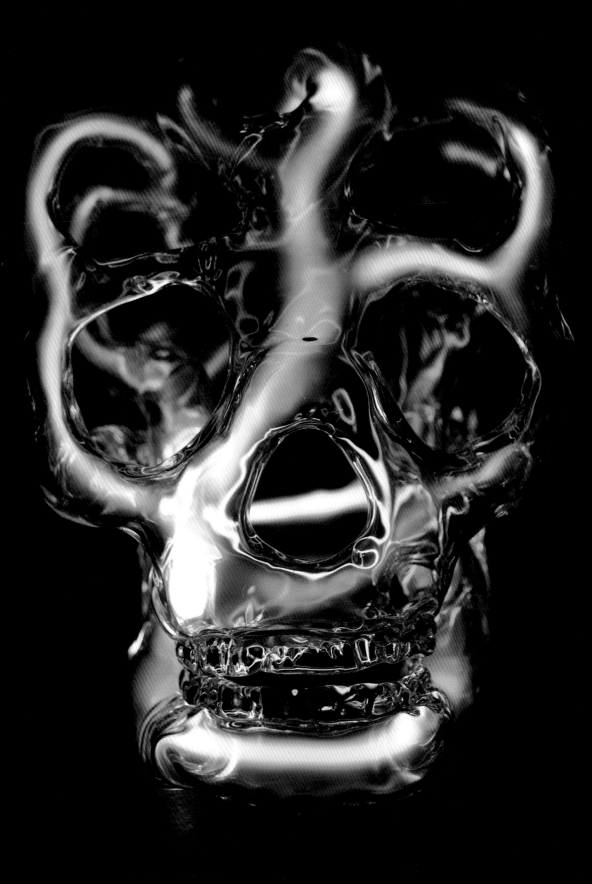

Sculptor Franklin reveals something of his painstaking process:

"To preserve the luminosity of the krypton, every glass seal has to be perfect. And each piece contains hundreds. If one rogue molecule gets inside the void of the glass tubing it contaminates the gas, and will no longer glow. There are times when the holes in the seals are so small that you cannot actually see them with your eyes – without the help of a leak detector."

Opposite and right
Skull #2

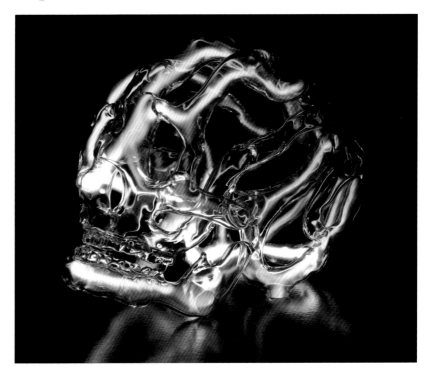

The sealing process for Eric Franklin's series of sculptures often results in misshapen areas, which become part of the final artwork.

His disembodied skulls gently glow, suggestive of the one quality they do not possess – life.

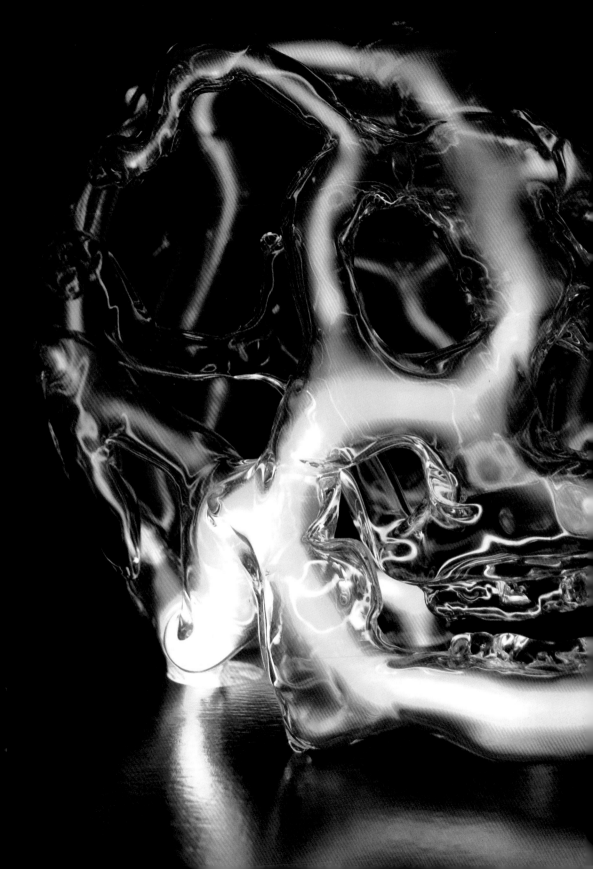

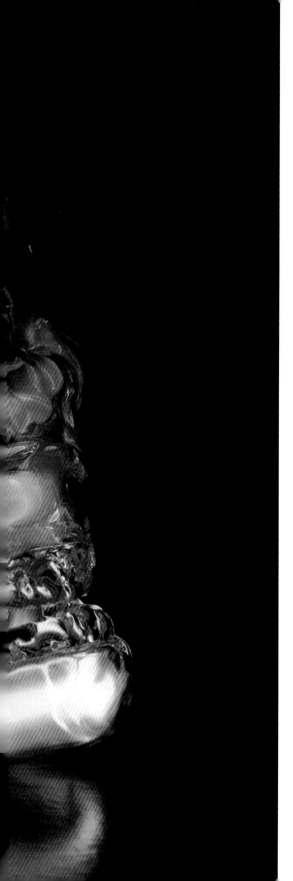

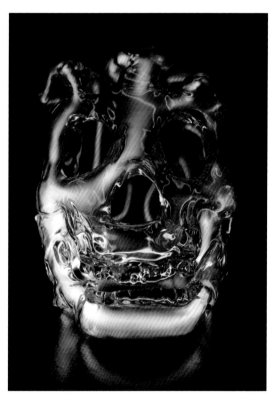

Skull #3

FELT MISTRESS

Felt Mistress, AKA Louise Evans, is a UK-based stitcher and prolific tea drinker. Originally trained in fashion design and millinery (hats!), Louise brings couture dressmaker skills to the world of character design. In collaboration with her partner, illustrator Jonathan Edwards, and others (Jon Burgerman, Jon Knox, Pete Fowler . . .) she creates a zoo-full of one-off bespoke creatures. Main interests: sewing, Japan, buttons, French Fancies and Mr Edwards.

Look for her monograph *Felt Mistress: Creature Couture*, from Blank Slate Books.

www.feltmistress.com

Top left
Marcel

Opposite
FMSkull

406

JUD TURNER

Living and working in the same place where he was born, Eugene, Oregon, on the USA's West Coast, sculptor Jud Turner focuses on direct-welded steelwork, re-purposed consumer items, and found object assemblages. "A high premium was placed on education and creativity when I was growing up. I have always drawn, painted, sculpted – tried to make some sort of tangible record of my experiences and impressions of the world around me."

Bottom left
Killing Time, 2007,
26 x 12 x 10 in. welded steel,
found objects, mahogany
wood base

Opposite
*Eat Your Veggies (so that
one day the veggies may eat
you)*, 2009 , 32 x 26 x 12 in.
(wall hanging) found object
assemblage

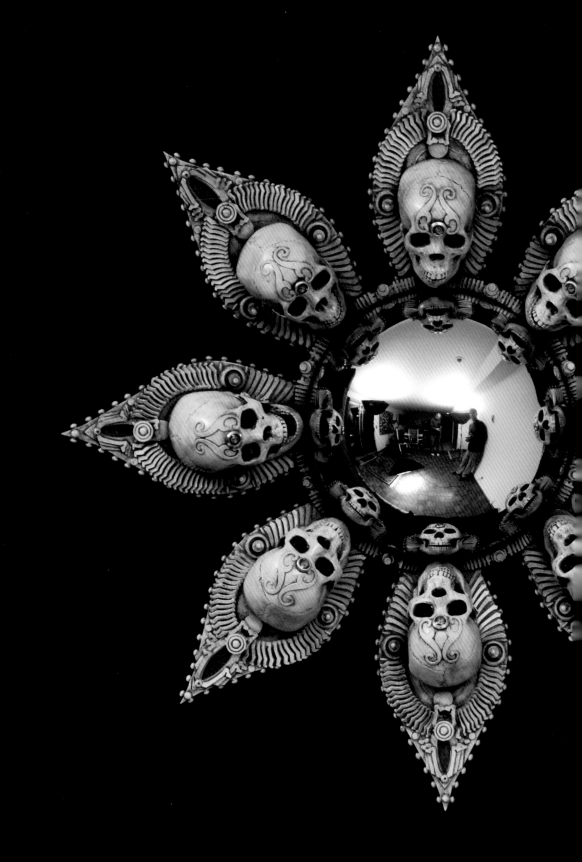

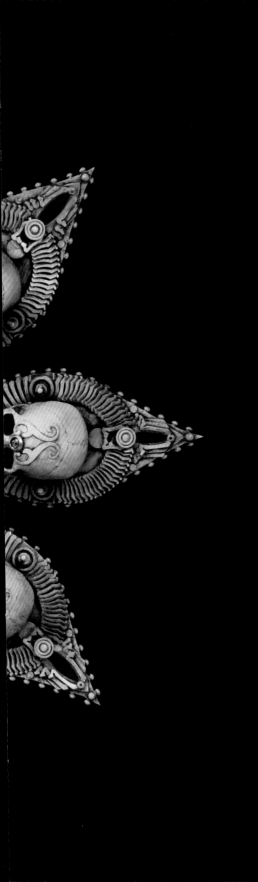

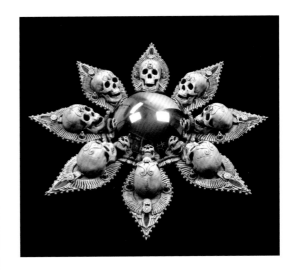

Lotus Eaters, 2011,
50 x 16 in. mixed media
assemblage (wall hanging)

"There are few areas in one's life where true freedom is available; art is where I am able to find true freedom."

Jud Turner

Placing a high value on craftsmanship, Turner creates artworks about the exhilarations and anxieties of living in our modern, industrialized society. "My work is an attempt to engage viewers on several levels of visual perception; I make art that is fun to look at, but my sculptures can have disturbing implications and mixed meanings."

Says Turner: "The themes addressed in my work are contemporary issues that many of us ponder: mortality, the intersection of nature and technology, the passing of time, spirituality, and environmental sustainability. I spend as much time as possible welding, working and laughing."

Bottom and Opposite
Rose, 2013,
40 x 50 x 20 in.
found object assemblage,
welded steel (100% recycled
materials)

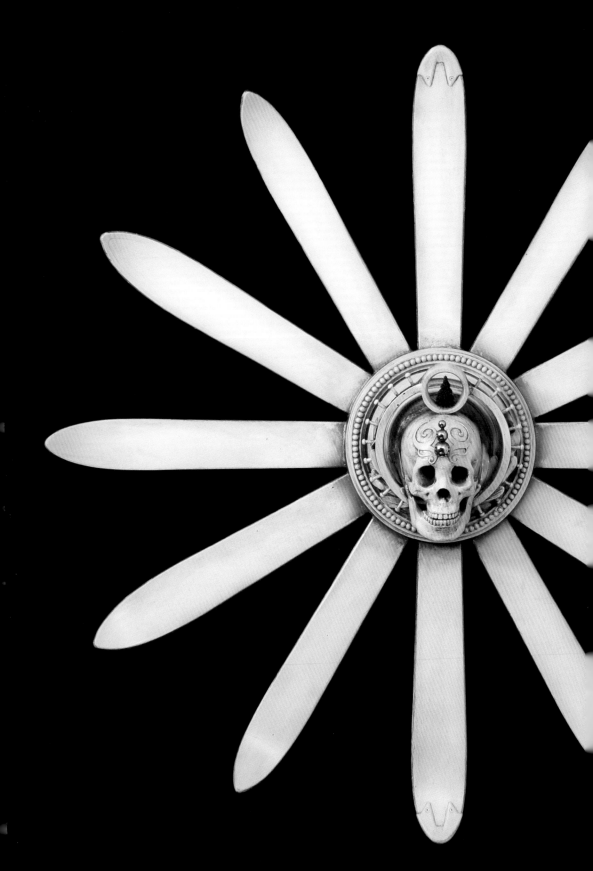

STOLEN ART!

This sculpture was stolen during an elaborate break-in at the Matter Gallery in Olympia, Washington. If you see this sculpture or have any information on its whereabouts, please contact the Olympia Police Department. Death to theft!

Opposite and Above
Tribute to the Concussed Skier, 2010, 48 x 10 in.
wall hanging found object assemblage

SKULLPTURE

The Thirteenth Skull,
2009, 34 x 10 in.
(wall hanging). Found object
assemblage created in the
tradition of "memento mori"

Morte Concubitu,
2010, 33 x 10 in.
wall hanging found object
assemblage.

Exciting prospects for 2014 include a steampunk-themed show in Seoul, South Korea, and an invitation from the CIA (Cambridge International Arts!) to create a sculpture for the Tour de France.

www.judturner.com

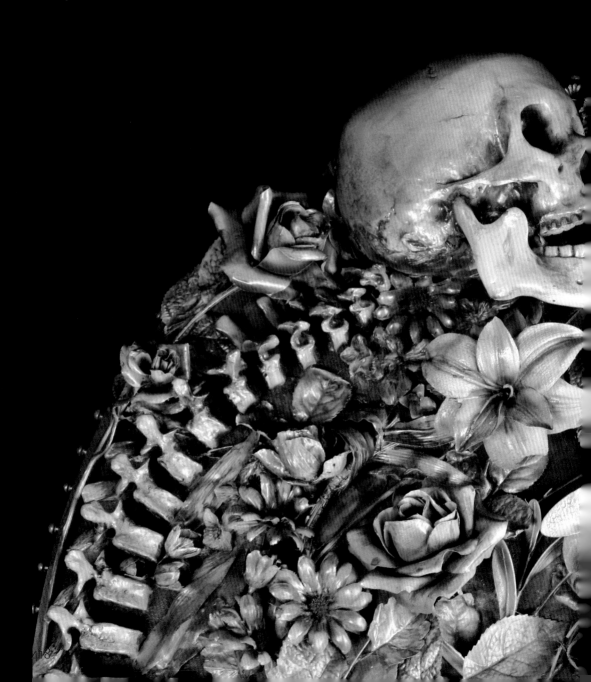

CONJURER'S KITCHEN

Welcome to the Conjurer's Kitchen, where *chef d'horreur* Annabel de Vetten (aka Annabel Lecter) performs her own special brand of culinary wizardry: cakes, treats, meats and oddities that aren't to everyone's taste . . . around her work, the phrase you're most likely to hear is, "That's edible!?"

Retiring from a very successful painting career several years ago, Annabel instead set her sights on the growing world of Cake Art, her unique work immediately grabbing attention – in both food and art worlds! Her devilish sense of humour and macabre leanings have made her unusual and creatively custom-decorated cakes a favourite, not only among people with a yen for the unusual, but also celebrities, television and movie producers, as well as earning her a prominent place in *Ripley's Believe It or Not.*

"The more unusual the request, the happier we are. Nothing is too weird for the Conjurer's Kitchen!" Annabel Lecter

www.conjurerskitchen.com

Top left
Conjurer Annabel puts the finishing touch to an upside-down cake.

Opposite
'Til Death Do Us Part (Skullcake Kittens); *felis catus,* cacao, plus barn owl, carrion crow and monkey skulls in chocolate.

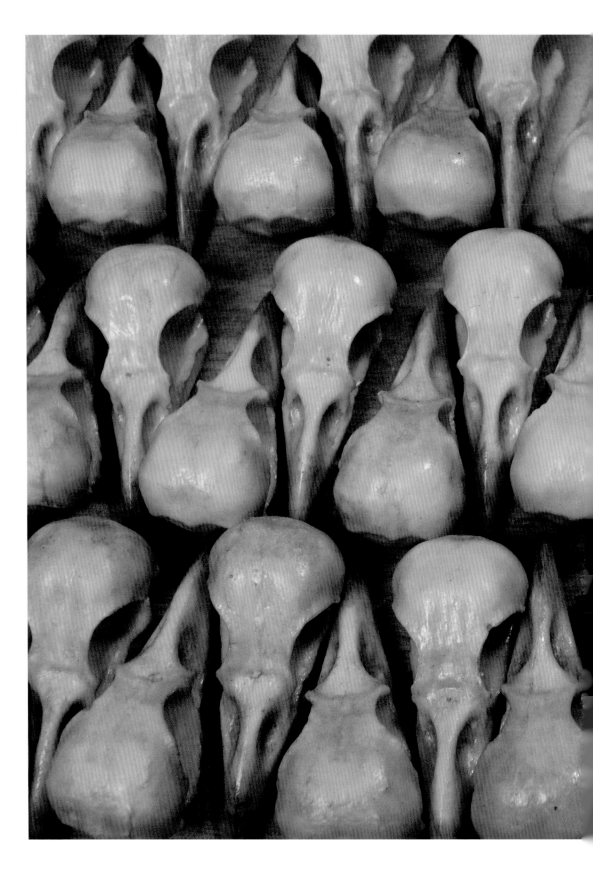

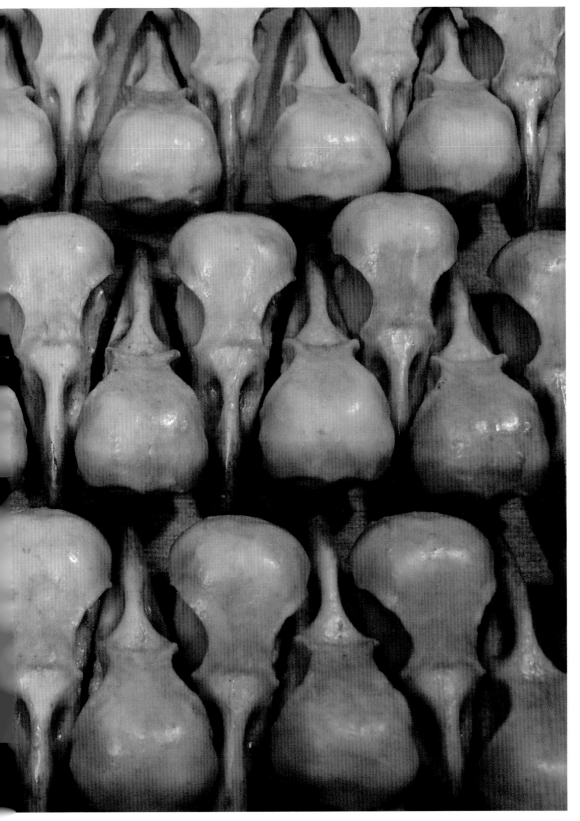

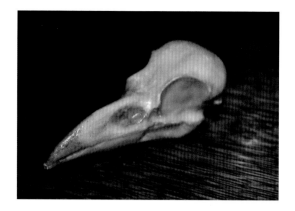

Previous spread and top
White chocolate Crow Skulls,
Corvus Corone, cacao.

Right
Conjoined Vervet Monkey
Skulls, Filigree Monkeys

Opposite top
Nigel, Death in Chocolate,
Handmade, hand painted
skull – life size, 100%
chocolate and 100% edible

Following spread
Tentacle Skull cake,
Cake and chocolate skull
combination made for, and
with, Kraken Rum

Below
Viking cake

Opposite
Edible Vanitas Case,
a collaboration between
Annabel de Vetten,
Tasha Marks and David
Bradley. Mixed media
including chocolate, sugar,
marshmallows, apples,
pears and ambergris
46 x 30 x 21 cm.
www.avmcuriosities.com
Photo: Chelsea Bloxsome

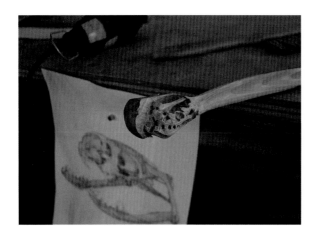

MASKULL LASSERRE

Maskull Lasserre, born in Calgary, Alberta, spent his early childhood in South Africa, before returning to Canada where his family has settled in the Ottawa area. He studied visual art and philosophy (BFA) at Mount Allision University, and sculpture (MFA) at Concordia University. Lasserre's drawings and sculptures explore the unexpected in the everyday, elements of the macabre that imbue the familiar with new strangeness. Awarded several public sculpture commissions, he is represented in the collections of the Musée des Beaux-arts de Montréal, the Government of Canada, and the Canada Council for the Arts. Maskull is also a recent participant in the Canadian Forces War Artist Program in Afghanistan.

www.maskulllasserre.com

Secret Carpentry, 2011
Carved axe,
27 x 6 x 2 in.

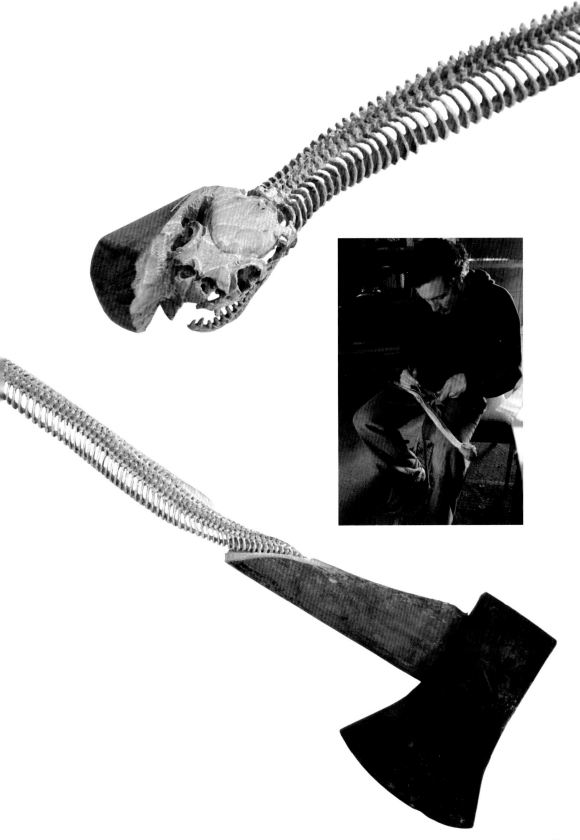

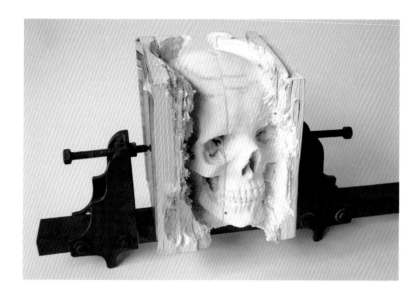

Incarnate (private collection)
Human skull carved into old
software manuals, 2012
Books, steel, hardware
40 x 8 x 11 in.

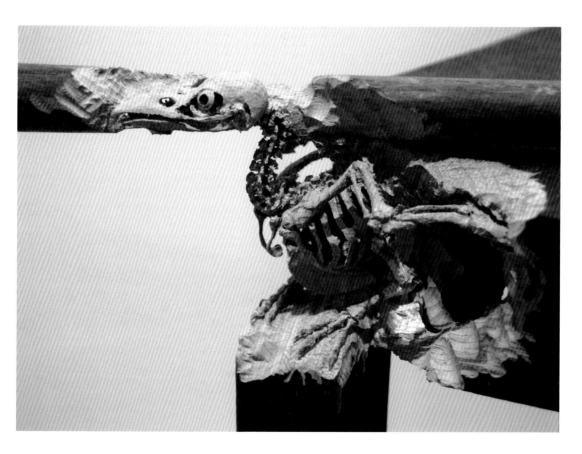

Fable, 2012
Young crow skeleton carved
into a chair and axe
26 x 23 x 37 in.

Rat, 2012
Rat skeleton carved into
a door and rolling-pin
38 x 14 x 80 in.

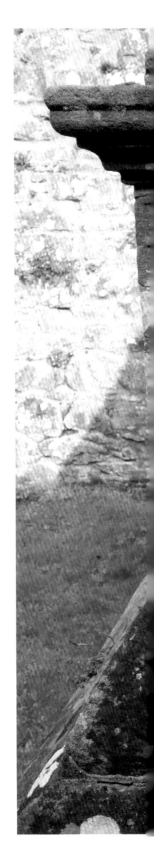

GRAVEYARD, ANWOTH

One of the finest cult films ever made is *The Wicker Man* (1973), starring screen legend Christopher Lee*. A peculiarly pagan British horror movie, directed by Robin Hardy and written by playwright Anthony (*Equus*) Shaffer, over the decades it has gathered a huge and devoted fanbase.

Martin Griffin set himself the task of tracking down all of the film's various original locations along Scotland's south-west coast, making up the storyline's mythical remote island of Summerisle. Among these many is Anwoth Old Kirk (Church of Scotland).

"When you walk around the graveyard you do feel sadness because of all the children and young adults that died so young." Martin Griffin

www.wickermanpilgrim.com

*One of the worst films ever made is *The Wicker Man* (2006), starring Nicolas Cage's teeth and hair. Avoid! The original has been re-released in a brand new definitive cut, with restored footage – It is time to keep your appointment with The Wicker Man. Photograph by Martin Griffin

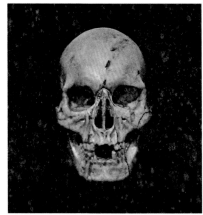

WHEN IN ROME

A Photo Journal by Rian Hughes

On a recent visit to Rome, British graphic designer, illustrator and comics artist Rian Hughes was primed and on the look out for likely skulls. In a city steeped in culture and rich with history, he couldn't fail to come up trumps. Carved, engraved or sculpted, everywhere you turn, there's a silent presence, watching . . .

All photographs: Rian Hughes

www.devicefonts.co.uk
www.cult-ure.net

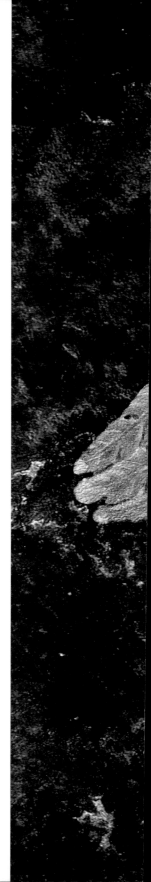

ACKNOWLEDGEMENTS

Many hearty and deathless thanx to the following, without whose generous help and advice this book would not have been possible:

Duncan Proudfoot, Gregory Benton, Erica Smith, Skull Empress Rebecca Snotflower, Dominic Regan, Niamh Coghlan, Nicky Peacock, Vicki Rawlinson, Maria Domenica, Jessica Joslin, Mark Stafford, Randy Franklin, Claire Richardson, Crown Prince of Skulls Noah Scalin, Emperor of Death Paul Koudounaris, Skullfinder General Søren Mosdal, King of Skulls Emek, Estagiário da Vandal, Roger Jolley, Kiyoshi Nakazawa, Paul O'Connell, Xtina Lamb, Leo at Skullis.

All apologies to those that I had to leave out this time –
ILYA, Dead Ed

Set your browsers for stun:

Recommended sites for your daily hit of hot skull action:

www.skulladay.blogspot.co.uk

www.skullis.com

www.iwantyourskull.com

www.skullappreciationsociety.com

Opposite
James Harvey (for Jamie Smart), Corporate Skull. Here's lookin' at you . . .

Following page
Death has the last laugh, Rian Hughes